PRAISE FROM PARENTS

"Dr. Turecki's understanding and knowledge of children with difficult temperaments is astounding."

"The Difficult Child Program taught me to be a better parent to my difficult child and also made me a better parent for my 'easy' child."

"Dr. Turecki's program has taught me the real meaning of motherhood."

PRAISE FROM PROFESSIONALS

"A clear and lucid prescription of how to deal with a difficult child. The compassionate understanding of the author is evident throughout."
—Irving Philips, M.D.,
Past President, American Academy of Child
Psychiatry

"A cornucopia of good ideas for assessing and intervening in these often disastrous relationship patterns."
—Donald A. Bloch, M.D.,
Director, The Ackerman Institute for Family Therapy

"A unique and extremely valuable book. I can recommend it enthusiastically."
—William B. Carey, M.D.,
Clinical Associate Professor of Pediatrics,
University of Pennsylvania School of Medicine

"This volume will sit on my shelf between Spock and Gesell."
—Richard L. Saphir, M.D.,
Associate Clinical Professor of Pediatrics,
The Mount Sinai School of Medicine

"Virtually every teacher has taught a child who is 'difficult' to handle. This book is invaluable in helping teachers and parents understand the roots of this behavior and thus, helping them cope more effectively."
—Ellen Galinsky,
Coauthor of The Preschool Years,
President, The Families and Work Institute

THE DIFFICULT CHILD

by Stanley Turecki, M.D.,
with Leslie Tonner

Revised Edition

BANTAM BOOKS
NEW YORK • TORONTO • LONDON • SYDNEY • AUCKLAND

THE DIFFICULT CHILD
A Bantam Book

PRINTING HISTORY
Bantam hardcover edition / October 1985
13 printings through March 1989
Revised Bantam trade edition / October 1989

Library of Congress Cataloging-in-Publication Data

Turecki, Stanley.
  The difficult child/by Stanley Turecki with Leslie Tonner—
Rev. ed.
     p.   cm.
  Bibliography: p.
  Includes index.
  ISBN 0-553-34446-3
  1. Problem children. 2. Child rearing. 3. Hyperactive
children. 4. Child psychology. I. Tonner, Leslie. II. Title.
HQ773.T87   1989
649'.153—dc20   87-47568
                                                CIP

Published simultaneously in the United States and Canada

Bantam Books are published by Bantam Books, a division of
Bantam Doubleday Dell Publishing Group, Inc. Its trademark,
consisting of the words "Bantam Books" and the portrayal of a
rooster, is Registered in U.S. Patent and Trademark Office and in
other countries. Marca Registrada. Bantam Books, 666 Fifth Ave-
nue, New York, New York 10103.

PRINTED IN THE UNITED STATES OF AMERICA
OPM   15   14   13   12   11   10   9

Contents

Do You Have a Difficult Child?

FAMILY QUESTIONS   Answer "YES" or "NO"

1. Do you find your child hard to raise?   └────┘

2. Do you find the child's behavior hard to
   understand?   └────┘

3. Are you often battling the child?   └────┘

4. Do you feel inadequate or guilty as a parent?   └────┘

5. Is your marriage or family life being affected
   by the child?   └────┘

CHILD QUESTIONS

The headings below identify possibly difficult areas of
your child's temperament (his or her basic makeup).
Rate your child, in an overall way, on each item, using
this scale:

   0 = No problem
   1 = Moderate problem
   2 = Definite problem
   3 = Extreme problem

High Activity Level
Very active, restless, fidgety; always into things;
makes you tired; "ran before he walked"; easily
overstimulated; gets wild or "revved up"; impulsive, loses control, can be aggressive; hates
to be confined.   └────┘

Distractibility
Has trouble concentrating and paying attention, especially if not really interested; doesn't
"listen"; tunes you out; daydreams; forgets instructions.   └────┘

High Intensity
Loud and forceful whether miserable, angry, or happy. ⌞⌟

Irregularity
Unpredictable. Can't tell when he'll be hungry or tired; conflict over meals and bedtime; wakes up at night; moods are changeable; has good or bad days for no obvious reason. ⌞⌟

Negative Persistence
Stubborn; goes on and on nagging, whining, or negotiating if wants something; relentless, won't give up; gets "locked in"; may have long tantrums. ⌞⌟

Low Sensory Threshold
"Sensitive"—physically not emotionally; highly aware of color, light, appearance, texture, sound, smell, taste, or temperature (not necessarily all of these); "creative," but with strong and unusual preferences that can be embarrassing; clothes have to feel and look right, making dressing a problem; doesn't like the way many foods look, smell, or taste; picky eater; bothered and overstimulated by bright lights and noisy settings; refuses to dress warmly when the weather is cold. ⌞⌟

Initial Withdrawal
Shy and reserved with new people; doesn't like new situations; holds back or protests by crying or clinging; may tantrum if forced to go forward. ⌞⌟

Poor Adaptability
Has trouble with transition and change of activity or routine; inflexible, very particular, notices minor changes; gets used to things and won't give them up; has trouble adapting to anything unfamiliar; can want the same clothes or foods over and over. ⌞⌟

Negative Mood
Basically serious or cranky; doesn't show pleasure openly; not a "sunny" disposition. ⌐___⌐

What Your Rating Means

FAMILY "YES"	CHILD	CONCLUSION
0–1	+ 3–5 points	= Some difficult features
2–3	+ 6–12 points	= Difficult child
4–5	+ 13 or more points	= Very difficult child

FOREWORD

One of the tests of a clinical concept is its exportability. Is it merely a private idea, usable only by those who devised it? Or does it have broader applicability?

Child development researchers have done considerable exploration of the significance of temperament in the interactional processes that unfold the world to the child, and the child to society. But the practical application of temperament research findings by child psychiatrists has as yet not been widely attempted, or at least has not been widely reported. This book begins to fill the gap.

Dr. Stanley Turecki was not among those engaged in the original inquiry into temperament and its many facets that goes by the title of the New York Longitudinal Study (NYLS), and the concept of the "difficult" child as used in this book is not identical to that used in the NYLS researches. But it is totally within the spirit of the NYLS, and Dr. Turecki has followed closely our definitions of the individual temperamental qualities.

The New York Longitudinal Study was born some thirty years ago to Dr. Alexander Thomas and myself, two psychiatrists who found the theories of the time both incomplete and inaccurate. As clinicians, Dr. Thomas, working with adults, and I, working with children and adolescents, were troubled by the simplistic and insufficiently supported concepts that assigned to parental handling and attitudes—most especially those of the mother —the blame and responsibility for a host of child behavior disorders. That there could be difficulties between parents and a child, a teacher and a pupil, between peers and a child; this was all too evident. Some children had trouble only in certain situations, while in other children difficulties appeared to be ubiquitous. But that noxious maternal handling was always or even most often the primary cause, so that the mother was the culprit, seemed to defy many of the facts of the specific situations. Besides being inaccurate, such explanations saddled innumerable mothers with anxiety and guilt, without giving them clear-cut guidance as to how to change for the better. These considerations led us in 1956 to start a long-term study. Such a study had to start when the children were very young infants, before anyone knew which child would show difficulties later on. This is what we did, and we are still following the NYLS group, now that they are young adults.

In our explorations, we found that temperamental qualities could be distinguished in children from early infancy on and that these qualities had their own effects upon parents and others. Consequently, the child's temperament influenced the parents' behavior and attitude, just as the parents influenced their children. It was a two-way street, not always one way from parent to child. We also found that any one kind of parental handling, even with the best of intentions, worked well with some children but not with others. The results depended not only on what the parents did but also on the child's temperament. To be in the best interests of the child, parental handling needed to take the child's temperamental individualities into account. We also identified one combination of temperamental qualities that seemed to bring about proportionately more difficult management of the child. This we named the "difficult child" cluster.

Dr. Turecki has expanded the meaning of the term but maintained the spirit in which it was coined. He has found that for some parents, particular temperamental characteristics are particularly trying; these may or may not be those of the research "difficult child" combination. For example, high distractibility may drive some parents up the wall, or the child with low sensory threshold who complains about food tastes or the feel of clothing may turn meals and dressing into intolerable confrontations. For these parents, such children are "difficult," even though other qualities that we labeled "difficult" in our research might bother them less. So, as a true clinician, Dr. Turecki set about defining for individual parents and children the temperamental factors that made for difficulty. He also set about finding concrete management techniques that would minimize the unhappy consequences of the child's behavior while preserving for the child the ability to mature, to learn, and to adapt. As stormy and ineffectual interactions were replaced by productive ones consonant with the child's temperament, parents and children could learn to like and respect each other better.

Dr. Turecki has now put his clinical experience into a form useful to other clinicians, and most importantly, for the direct use of parents. The experience reported is with a variety of types of difficult children and their parents. Not all such children have psychiatric problems. For these youngsters, the term "primary prevention" best expresses the service given, akin to the management of diet and habits utilized for primary prevention of heart disease.

The children and parents who appear in this book live in urban, Western society, and hence it may not be possible to generalize their situations and solutions unchanged beyond similar cultural circumstances. But that a good fit between parental handling and child temperament is vital to help children adapt to the imperatives of their society is a crucial concept that can be applied to other cultures.

Dr. Turecki has explained these ideas in a form that parents can easily understand, but without diluting the substance and meaning of this approach. His advice is sound, sensible, and practical and at the same time captures the essence of the vast research in this area over the past thirty years. I can recommend it highly.

STELLA CHESS, M.D.
Professor of Psychiatry
New York University School of Medicine

To my family,
with love and respect
and
To Roberta and Sol,
the special ones

A PERSONAL
INTRODUCTION

I am a child and family psychiatrist and the parent of an ex-difficult child. Jillian has developed into an interesting, popular, and very positive teenager, but her early years were a different story.

The year prior to her birth was a good one for our family. We were settled in New York City, our two daughters were in school, and my wife, Lucille, was pregnant. I had completed my training in adult and child psychiatry, was affiliated with a good hospital, and had entered private practice. Like so many young psychiatrists, I was still searching for a truly personal style. Two men in particular continued to influence me strongly.

Dr. Harry Weinstock, an eminent psychoanalyst and my immigration sponsor, always combined sound theory with straightforward practical thinking. I learned much, not only about my profession, but about life in general, from this elegant, worldly man. Dr. Sol Nichtern had supervised me during my training. Soon after starting in private practice, I entered into an association with him. First a pediatrician and then a child psychiatrist, he was widely respected in our profession. Kind and extremely perceptive, he understood children and their development like no other adult I have ever met. He taught me many valuable lessons—among them, to respond to the uniqueness of people, and never to underestimate their strengths.

Jillian arrived on a cold winter morning in early 1974. Within a day the head nurse in the newborn nursery remarked: "That one is going to be trouble." A restless, irritable baby, totally unpredictable in her feeding and sleeping, she always seemed to be screaming. Neither Lucille, an experienced mother, nor a baby-nurse could soothe her. Sleepless nights were the rule in our home, so that by the time Jillian was six months old, Lucille was exhausted and we were both tense—not a good situation for our two older daughters. The pediatrician assured us that the baby was normal, but at times her erratic behavior made this hard to believe. With the advice of Sol Nichtern, Lucille was able to impose some schedules. Eventually, with considerable strain on all, we came through Jillian's infancy.

By the time she was 2, Jillian, with Lucille's continuing efforts, had settled into somewhat more predictable routines. Still, when Jillian was upset, a very loud, very long tantrum usually followed. Often it was hard to understand why she had such extreme reactions. Dressing her, bedtime, going for a walk—virtually any new experience—could cause problems. My training and experience as a child psychiatrist helped somewhat, but all too often, I found myself reacting as a bewildered parent. We were finding it hard to discipline her; but we were also gradually learning to accept at least some of her behavior.

At about this time, in my efforts to understand my child and her puzzling reactions, I reread *Temperament and Behavior Disorders in Children*, a book by Drs. Stella Chess and Alexander Thomas about their New York Longitudinal Study of temperament. Suddenly there it was: the erratic eating and sleeping, the "unhappiness," the negative reactions to anything new, the problems with transition and change, the loudness; all were there. I studied the book carefully, looking for ideas on dealing with Jillian's behavior.

The next three years, until Jillian started elementary school, were better, but not consistently so. We were still sometimes puzzled, but we could now understand more of the behavior as an expression of Jillian's temperament. We learned to create routines whenever possible, and Jillian thrived on these. We tried to avoid unfamiliar situations, and when we couldn't, Lucille would prepare her carefully. Strengths were emerging. Jillian could be extremely funny. She had a wonderful imagination. She loved to dress up and play games with her dolls. She was going to a carefully selected nursery school with warm, accepting teachers who obviously liked her. Lucille now had some time to herself.

Problem areas remained. Jillian was at her most difficult with Lucille. Occasional tantrums in the park and other public places still caused embarrassment. Good days at school were followed by struggles at home. With many gains we would notice a slipback in another area. She could be charming and delightful in the afternoon but cranky and fearful the same evening; excited about going to a birthday party but then refuse to leave Lucille's side when they arrived. Jillian was more trouble than our two older daughters combined, but she was such an *interesting* child that life was never dull with her.

Professionally my whole focus was shifting. No longer did I view problem behavior in young children as only a reaction to their parents or as a developmental "phase." I was now asking more and more questions about the child's temperament. "What is this child really like? What kind of person is she? Is she hard to raise? How does she affect her family?" I clearly started to see that many parent-child problems were *not* caused by the parents alone. Of course, the parents' personalities were important and impacted on their children, but this was a two-way street, with traffic flowing in both directions. And in many cases the child's contribution deserved more attention.

By 1982, Jillian was doing well in elementary school, much better at home, and loved going to summer sleep-away camp. (More about her progress in the conclusion of this book.) And I had found that my experience as her father, together with my increasing sophistication about temperament-related issues, was allowing me to work with the families of difficult children in a much more meaningful way.

At the end of the year, my friend Dr. Herbert Porter arranged for me to talk about my work to the pediatricians at Lenox Hill Hospital in New York City. I asked

Lucille to participate and to share with the doctors her experience as the mother of a difficult child. The presentation was received with interest, and the director, Dr. Edward Davies, encouraged me to continue my efforts to reach more pediatricians. A year later, Dr. Richard Bonforte, Director of Pediatrics at Beth Israel Hospital, where I was an attending child psychiatrist, invited me to present at pediatric grand rounds. Once again, Lucille participated. The President of the hospital, Dr. Robert Newman, happened to be present. He asked if the mothers of such children would benefit from being in support groups. A plan began to crystallize: a program for the families of difficult children.

I could provide evaluation and guidance for the parents, and Lucille could lead the support groups. If more help was needed, my professional experience would allow me to offer further help to an individual member of the family, the couple, or the entire family. I wrote a proposal and took it to the director of the Department of Psychiatry, Dr. Arnold Winston. He accepted the concept immediately and has provided continued support. I will always be grateful to him.

Thus the Difficult Child Program was born, under the joint sponsorship of the departments of Psychiatry and Pediatrics. The program grew quickly. By mid-1984 we were busy enough for me to train another professional, Carole Sands, in the principles and techniques of working with the families of difficult children.

In 1985 I founded the Difficult Child Center based in my private practice in Manhattan, and recruited another professional, Steven Friedfeld. Both Carole, a clinical psychologist, and Steve, a certified social worker, are highly respected in their fields and have made a significant contribution. Ruth Johnson, my secretary and assistant, has provided a most welcoming atmosphere for the families that come to the Difficult Child Center.

My strong desire to help more parents with hard-to-raise children led naturally to the writing of this book. Leslie Tonner, a writer and herself a mother, participated actively in the writing of the original manuscript. Her technical knowledge, quick grasp of the issues, and ability to portray day-to-day situations were most helpful. My editor at Bantam Books, Toni Burbank, has been essential to the book's success. Always available and strongly committed, she has provided continuing guidance and support.

Since *The Difficult Child* was first published in 1985, I have continued to learn from the parents of difficult children. I have received thousands of letters and continue to interact with parents in my practice. I very much enjoy the questions and answers that follow my lectures to parents and professionals. All this feedback has enabled me to refine my thinking and develop new techniques. This knowledge is incorporated in the extensive revisions I have made for this paperback edition of my book.

Personally, in my dual role of parent and professional, I have found the writing of *The Difficult Child* immensely rewarding. I hope that it will add to our clinical body of knowledge and prove helpful to many professionals who come into contact with difficult children.

In the final analysis, however, I have written this book for you, the parents. It is my most sincere hope that it will prove helpful to you so that you in turn can help your difficult child realize her or his full individual potential. May you soon look to your child's future with optimism, anticipation, and confidence.

STANLEY TURECKI, M.D.
March 1989

PART I

SOME CHILDREN ARE BORN DIFFICULT

1

DO YOU KNOW
THIS CHILD?

Matthew has trouble going to sleep at night and staying asleep. Trying to get him to go to bed in his own room can provoke a pitched battle. Matthew has been a poor sleeper since infancy. And even though he has a night-light, and a collection of stuffed animals, he often ends up coming into his parents' bed several times during the night. If it's very late, his mother lets him climb in; her husband always argues with her about the wisdom of this, but they cannot break the child's habit. He also has problems with eating. His mother continually pushes good, nutritious food at him, which he always rejects, saying he doesn't like it. He can be funny and he draws beautifully, but most of the time he is a serious, cranky child. He doesn't like to spend time alone. He interrupts his mother when she's trying to talk on the phone, and doesn't let his parents hold a private conversation.

When not battling Matthew, his mother feels guilty and sorry for him. She knows she should be firmer, but if she or his father try to stop him from coming into their room or try to get him to sit at the table and eat properly, poor little 4-year-old Matthew throws loud, long tantrums. They'll do anything to keep him from doing that, even give up their privacy in bed. But it's all getting to be a bit much for this family. They feel controlled by their child and disagree on how best to deal with him. The marriage is showing strain. The older brother, John, is complaining that he never gets any attention and that Matthew bosses him around.

◆

"I can't believe this is my kid," Brian's mother often says. She is precise and orderly. Her 5-year-old has been on the go since he could crawl; the house is *never* neat in spite of her best efforts. Although Brian can pay attention for a while to TV or his puzzles, he is usually moving from one thing to another and can't sit still. Whether laughing or crying he is always very loud. He gets revved up very easily, especially in a noisy room filled with people or in brightly lit stores and markets. In the playground he gets overexcited and can push or hit other children. His mother is very embarrassed by such behavior but finds it hard to be firm because she's not sure of herself and Brian just "doesn't listen." He doesn't need much sleep, and it's hard to put him to bed at night, leaving little time for the parents to be alone.

In kindergarten the teachers think of Brian as a troublemaker and have alluded to possible "hyperactivity" because he is always on the go and sometimes loses control. Brian's pediatrician, who sees the child in his busy, crowded office, agrees and has raised the possibility of medication.

His parents, and especially his mother, are confused and worried. She has recently returned to work, and wonders whether this has anything to do with Brian's problems. When the school or the baby-sitter call with the "incident of the day," her stomach tightens into a knot. Brian has been saying, "I'm bad," and his generally sunny disposition is being replaced by an angry, surly attitude.

◆

Isabel is an adorable 4-year-old with blond curls, green eyes, and a peaches and cream complexion. She is generally an easy child who plays by herself and goes to sleep without much fuss. She has a circle of friends and does well in school. She seems to be a model child, but if you talk to her mother you get a different story. "I don't know what's the matter with her," she says. "She's so adorable, but when she decides she doesn't want to wear something or eat something or do something, I can't

make her change her mind. She is the most stubborn
and willful child alive then, and if I try to insist, she will
just go on and on like a broken record. She is absolutely
relentless when she wants something." What sets Isabel
off? "She won't wear anything that isn't pale purple or
pink," her mother says with exasperation. "She won't
wear turtlenecks, or bib overalls, or socks." And why
does Isabel reject these items? Because, her mother will
tell you, they don't "feel right." And as a result, Isabel
has in her closet only a select, few items to dress in, no
socks and only tights, loose shirts and pants with draw-
string waists, no elastic. She wants to wear funny combinations, like polka-dot pink pants with a purple shirt.
And Isabel's mother, well groomed and fashion-conscious,
has been stuck with hundreds of dollars of unworn
clothing.

An administrator in a large company, she super-
vises fifty employees. Why then, she asks herself, can't
she get her 4-year-old to listen to her? Isabel also refuses
to eat many foods, sticking to the few she likes, and they
cannot take her out to eat unless the restaurant serves
fried chicken or peanut butter and jelly. Efforts to make
her dress more "normally" for school or to eat a proper
breakfast result in protracted negotiations, arguments,
sometimes even in screaming matches. And as if this
weren't enough, Isabel always seems to complain to her
mother about the way things look and feel and smell.
Her mother has to spend extra time helping Isabel find
things to wear, eat, and play with that don't "bother
her." Adorable Isabel is driving her mother crazy. And
Isabel is getting touchier and more stubborn with her
mother every day.

✦

In Rachel's house, Rachel's father privately refers to
his daughter as "the queen" because "she always gets
her way." He doesn't understand why his wife has to
give in to the child all the time. "She's just doing this to
get attention," he believes. In fact, Rachel is a shy,
rather rigid, and very stubborn child, who also knows

how to manipulate. She cries, whines, and clings fiercely to her mother. Her father feels his wife encourages this behavior. "Just give her a good whack when she does that," he keeps insisting. But Rachel can do more than just cry and cling. She will, at times, publicly tantrum, and her mother does not know how to handle that. She stands by helplessly as her child "makes a scene." Simple transitions from one activity to another can cause power struggles—for example, leaving the TV to come to the dinner table, putting on her coat to go out, or leaving the playground can result in trouble. If she wants something, she can go on and on nagging. She won't take no for an answer. When not battling her mother, she seems clinging and fearful.

By midafternoon, Rachel's mother is worn out from the fighting, and she alternately gives in or punishes Rachel, depending on how tired she herself is. She feels she is neglecting her 1-year-old. She is a somewhat timid person. She knows she is too involved and is not being effective, but she feels trapped.

The doctor pronounced Rachel a "terrible two," but now at 3½ no improvement is in sight. Rachel's father doesn't understand how a 3-year-old can cause so much trouble and believes his wife is responsible. Her mother feels angry, inadequate, and victimized.

◆

If you recognize your child in one of these vignettes, or, after completing the questionnaire, suspect for other reasons that your infant or child is indeed "difficult," then you need to know these basic facts:

• **Difficult children are normal.** They are *not* emotionally disturbed, mentally ill, or brain damaged. Well-meaning relatives or other parents may have suggested that "something must be wrong with him." You may have worried a lot about this yourself. So let's get a new perspective. "Difficult" is very different from "abnormal."

• *Difficult children are like this because of their innate makeup.* And that makeup is their inborn *temperament.* They are not like this because of something you as parents have done to them. It's not your fault. And it's not the child's fault, either. He didn't ask to be born difficult.

• *Difficult children are hard to raise.* Of course, you know this already. But if you think of it as a basic fact of existence, it will help you cope better. This is the way your child *is,* but by understanding him better and learning about his temperament you will be able to manage him successfully. He will then be a great deal easier to raise.

• *Difficult children are not all the same.* The picture differs depending on which areas of temperament come into play. Difficult children also range from the basically easy child with some difficult features, to the extreme of the very difficult, perhaps even impossible child.

• *Difficult children make their parents feel angry, inadequate, or guilty.* And these parental feelings can lead to one of the biggest problems with difficult children, that of ineffective discipline. Parents feel that they have lost their authority and that their child no longer "listens" to them. And this leads to a redoubling of disciplinary efforts, often to no avail.

• *Difficult children can create marital strain, family discord, problems with siblings, and end up with emotional problems of their own.*

or

• *Difficult children can become positive, enthusiastic, perhaps even especially creative individuals if they are well managed when young.* And teaching you how to do this is the goal of this book.

The first and most basic issue you should understand about your child is that of temperament, and how your child's individual temperamental traits shape his behavior from a very early age.

WHAT IS TEMPERAMENT?

Temperament is the natural, inborn style of behavior of each individual. It's the *how* of behavior, not the why. It should not be confused with motivation. The question is not, "*Why* does he behave a certain way if he doesn't get a cookie?" but rather, "When he doesn't get a cookie, *how* does he express his displeasure? Does he pout? Does he whine or complain? Or does he kick and scream?" This style of behavior is innate and is not produced by the environment. The environment—and your behavior as a parent—can influence temperament and interplay with it, but it is not the cause of temperamental characteristics.

Every child has his or her own temperament, which is a constellation of nine characteristics or traits. These were first defined by Drs. Alexander Thomas, Stella Chess, and Herbert Birch of New York University in their ground-breaking New York Longitudinal Study. This project, begun in 1956 and still ongoing, has followed 133 persons from infancy to young adulthood. Its objectives were to identify the individual temperamental characteristics of each child, and to follow these as the children developed and interacted with their environments. The nine temperamental traits are:

1. *Activity level.* How active or restless is the child generally, from an early age?
2. *Distractibility.* How easily is the child distracted? Can he pay attention?
3. *Intensity.* How loud is the child generally, whether happy or unhappy?
4. *Regularity.* How predictable is the child in his patterns of sleep, appetite, bowel habits?
5. *Persistence.* Once involved with something, does the child stay with it for a long time? (Positive persistence) How relentless or stubborn is he when he wants something? (Negative persistence)

6. *Sensory threshold.* How does the child react to sensory stimuli: noise, bright lights, colors, smells, pain, warm weather, tastes, the texture and feel of clothes? Is he easily bothered? Is he easily overstimulated?
7. *Approach/withdrawal.* What is the child's initial response to newness—new places, people, foods, clothes?
8. *Adaptability.* How does the child deal with transition and change?
9. *Mood.* What is the child's basic disposition? Is it more sunny or more serious?

By understanding these nine traits any given child's temperament may be classified in each area on a range from very easy to very difficult.

Take, for example, a child's innate activity level. In general, the more active he is the more difficult he will be to manage. And it follows, of course, that the more traits fall on the difficult end of the spectrum, the harder it becomes to raise the child.

THE TEMPERAMENTALLY DIFFICULT CHILD

In a general way any child can be assessed in each area as follows:

TEMPERAMENTAL TRAIT	EASY	DIFFICULT
Activity level	Low	High
Distractibility	Low	High
Intensity	Low	High
Regularity	Regular	Irregular
Negative Persistence	Low	High
Sensory threshold	High	Low
Approach/withdrawal	Approach	Withdrawal
Adaptability	Good	Poor
Mood	Positive	Negative

Depending on how many areas of temperament fall on the difficult end of the spectrum, and to what extent the resulting behavior poses a problem for the parents, any given family may be dealing with a child who is:

- *Basically easy but with some difficult features:* The parents are coping but may need to learn some management techniques and principles of discipline.

- *Difficult:* The child is hard to raise and there is strain on the mother and usually on the family.

- *Very difficult:* Both the child and the family are in trouble.

- *Impossible, a "mother-killer":* This graphically descriptive term says it all.

THEN WHAT DO YOU MEAN, HE'S NORMAL?

If you have a truly difficult child, you may have wondered if he could behave the way he does and still be "normal."

I strongly believe that you don't have to be average in order to be normal. Nor are you abnormal simply because you are difficult. To me abnormality implies the presence of a clear diagnosable disorder. Human beings are all different, and a great variety of characteristics and behaviors falls well into the range of normality.

Take, for example, three equally intelligent and motivated 8-year-olds sitting down to homework. One will work evenly and with good concentration; the second will have trouble getting started, but once he does will be so persistent that it's hard to get him to stop; the third child will jump right in, without any hesitation, but will then be easily distracted and work in fits and starts. None of these three behavioral styles is more "normal" than the other. They are simply different.

There are many more difficult children than you might suspect. The New York Longitudinal Study identified 10 percent of the normal children they studied as difficult. Furthermore, the authors did not include high activity level, distractibility, negative persistence, and low sensory threshold in their definition of a difficult child. Estimating conservatively, another 10 percent of children would be difficult because of these characteristics. Thus we can arrive at a rough estimate that some 20 percent of all children under the age of 6 are temperamentally difficult and hard to raise. Based on current census figures, this means that between three and four million young children in the United States are difficult. And if we introduce the concept of a basically easy child with some difficult traits, we are talking about many, many more.

WHAT CAUSES A DIFFICULT TEMPERAMENT?

No one knows for sure what the cause is. There is definitely a genetic factor, as in the transmission of hair or eye color. I often ask parents of a difficult child to ask their own parents, "What was I like as a child?" They have been surprised to hear their mothers and fathers identify in them traits similar to those they have perceived in their offspring. This would seem to indicate that inheritance plays a role, and research on identical twins supports this conclusion, although we cannot say that there is a direct transmittal of each and every characteristic from parent to child.

It is also now quite clear that many personality traits have a biological component. Nature, we are starting to realize, is every bit as important as nurture. Genetic influences, brain chemistry, and neurological development contribute strongly to who we are as children and what we become as adults. For example, tendencies to excessive worrying or timidity, leadership qualities, risk taking, obedience to authority, all appear to have a constitutional aspect.

The role of factors during the pregnancy is not clear. With highly active children, particularly those diagnosed as having "attention deficit hyperactivity disorder" one finds a somewhat greater incidence of pregnancy and delivery complications. And a high percentage of such children are boys. All other types of difficult children are as likely to be girls as boys.

There is no correlation between temperament and intelligence. Difficult children may be low, average, bright, or superior in their intellectual functioning. Nor is there any correlation with birth order or social class.

An intriguing association, not fully researched as yet, is between a difficult temperament and allergies, particularly food allergies. A certain number of difficult infants are allergic to milk. Later on they tend to have more ear and throat infections. Some parents notice a correlation between episodes of particularly difficult behavior and eating certain foods, especially those containing a lot of sugar or artificial additives. While the claims of the committed advocates of dietary approaches are generally viewed as exaggerated by the medical profession, many physicians believe in the link between nutrition and behavior; and certainly no one can argue with protecting our children from chemicals, pesticides, and other pollutants, and providing them with a diet most conducive to their healthy development.

Uneven neurological development may also be a factor. While most children do not always mature evenly, difficult children are usually more uneven. They may be very grown up, even advanced, in some ways—yet often act babyish and immature, leading to a general tendency to overreact. Impulse control, which depends on the maturation of certain parts of the brain, is often poor in highly active difficult children. Irregular sleep rhythms, late development of bladder control, and somewhat uneven language and learning skills development are not uncommonly seen in difficult children. Many of these children impress me as "high strung," skittish like finely bred racehorses. They are like this from an early age, often from infancy. All these features have to do with a child's neurophysiology.

I strongly recommend to parents, however, that they not become obsessed with the search for causes. The main thing for you to remember is that there is no evidence whatsoever that the way you parent your child *causes* his difficult temperament. Whatever the contributing factors, all children, including the difficult ones, are individuals not only in their physical characteristics and abilities but in their temperaments as well.

DO YOU MEAN MY CHILD ISN'T DOING THIS ON PURPOSE?

Precisely. Your child isn't being "bad" in order to "get" you. Unfortunately, it's common for parents to attribute motives to their children, especially if they are bewildered by the child's behavior. Lois, a young mother, felt extremely anxious each night when she made dinner because she never knew if her daughter Marcie would eat the meal or not. Lois began to believe that the harder she worked to prepare something her daughter liked, the quicker Marcie would reject the food, on purpose, because she knew her mother had worked so hard. Lois had not noticed, however, that toward the end of each day Marcie was hungry at a different hour—one night at 7:00 P.M., the next night at 9:00 P.M., the following afternoon at 4:30 P.M. Marcie's *irregular appetite* prevented her from sitting down each night at the same time, hungry. She wasn't trying to thwart her mother, she simply did not want to eat each night at 6:00 P.M. Of course, if Lois made a big fuss at mealtimes over whether Marcie sat down and ate her food, resulting in either bribery or a major fight, Marcie would come to see that not eating could be used as a tool to get her own way, and motivation would enter the picture.

THE VICIOUS CIRCLE

Difficult children tend to get locked into certain behavior patterns, but so do parents in response to the difficult behavior. This kind of repeated negative interaction may cause these traits in the child to become more pronounced.

Take another case, that of a small boy, Evan, who expressed an interest in owning a pair of roller skates and learning to skate. His father, eager to please Evan because the child normally did not express much pleasure or delight in anything, went out of his way to go to

several stores and buy the most expensive, flashy skates
he could find. When he brought the gift home and presented it to his son, Evan took it to his room with
scarcely any response. The father was furious. "How can
he do this to me! I went to four stores, I bought him the
best skates in the city." His son, in response to this
outburst from his father, threw the skates on the floor
and started to scream and cry. The father failed to realize that his son's disposition is due to his *negative mood*
and that a mild expression of pleasure from this child is
equal to another child crowing with delight. Evan is *not*
doing this on purpose because his father went to a lot of
trouble. This is Evan. But if his father continues to get
angry, eventually Evan's negative mood will be exaggerated by his father's response.

Difficult children, through their behavior, create a
"ripple effect" in their environment. Like a stone thrown
into a pond, the child's impact spreads in widening circles, affecting first the mother, then the rest of the
family, then the rest of his environment, like the extended family, neighbors, peers, and the school, although
these effects are less intense as the circles spread wider.

However, not only do difficult children affect their
environment, they in turn are themselves affected by
the responses of significant people around them. Not
understanding their difficult child's behavior, parents
cannot fall back on well-known methods of child-rearing
and discipline. Mothers become angry and guilty. Parents lose their authority. Ineffective discipline accentu-
ates even further the child's difficult behavior, in turn
increasing the power struggles. Eventually the whole
family becomes involved in the vicious circle, and to
some extent so can other people who interact with the
difficult child.

WEAR AND TEAR

How does this affect the child? Here the concept of "wear
and tear" is useful. As a result of the continuing friction,
the child may develop certain secondary problems. A
difficult child can become clinging and fearful. He may

have frequent nightmares or in general behave as if his feelings are easily hurt. Or he may act angry or spoiled much of the time.

Of most concern to me is the problem some of these children can develop with self-image. They behave as if they don't like themselves; they may actually say, "I'm bad." Lowered self-image may also show in other ways. Some children are too focused on winning or "coming out on top"; they often cheat at games. They are perfectionistic and easily frustrated. They can become very upset with themselves over small mistakes, or show great disappointment at minor setbacks. Paradoxically "spoiled" children, who behave like little tyrants at home, usually have a low self-esteem.

Such behavior is *not* determined by temperament but is frequently found in poorly managed difficult children. Once parents alter their management and the family atmosphere relaxes, this wear-and-tear behavior usually improves. In other words, it occurs in *reaction* to the vicious circle and is not indicative of deeper emotional problems.

However, if the vicious circle continues, eventually the child will be affected at a deeper level, and it is precisely these later emotional and behavioral problems that one is trying to prevent. This kind of *primary prevention* of future problems for both the child and other family members is perhaps the most basic goal of this book.

WHAT ARE DIFFICULT CHILDREN LIKE AT DIFFERENT AGES?

The expression of the difficult child's temperament varies at different ages. Some traits don't apply in infancy. Others intensify as the child gets older. The vicious circle and wear-and-tear effects on the child and family also increase with the age of the child.

Here are some examples of difficult traits at different ages. Remember that your child won't have every feature and that not every feature is evident in every situation.

Infants (Up to 12 Months)

It is not yet time for the power struggles between mother and child, but this period can be marked by exhaustion, marital strain, and some family tension. Most parents of a very difficult infant feel there is something wrong with the baby, especially if what may have been called "colic" doesn't get better by the fourth month. Some parents change pediatricians in their search for an answer.

> • *High activity level.* An extremely restless, squirmy, vigorous baby. (May even have been like this in utero.)
> • *Poor adaptability.* Reacts badly to changes in routine.
> • *Initial withdrawal.* Protests when first introduced to new foods, new places, or new people.
> • *High intensity.* Screams in distress or delight. A "loud baby."
> • *Irregularity.* Feeding and sleeping are very hard to schedule. An "unpredictable baby."
> • *Low sensory threshold.* Easily bothered by noises, lights, and texture of clothes. A sensitive, "jumpy baby."
> • *Negative mood.* Fusses, whimpers, or cries a great deal. An "unhappy baby."

Parents, in general, remember mostly the constant loud crying and the sleepless nights. Mothers often describe their infants as inconsolable.

A fuller description of difficult infants will be found in Chapter 10.

Children 12 to 48 Months

The child becomes more difficult to manage. This is the "terrible twos" with a vengeance. All children pass through a period of negativity and can be difficult to handle at this age. Much of this has to do with the child's developing identity, his first attempts to define himself as separate from his mother. Virtually every child goes through this phase; but with a difficult child this is not "just a phase" but rather a continuing expression of his temperament. Negative parental responses, marital strain, and family tension all increase. In a 3-year-old the difficult traits look like this:

• *High activity level.* This is more noticeable as the child becomes mobile. Parents are apt to say, "He ran before he walked"; the extremely active child is constantly on the go, gets revved up, and the house has to be thoroughly childproofed because the child is always getting into things. He gets overexcited and can become wild and lose control. He is impulsive and hates to be confined. His behavior may be noticed in nursery school, with peers, and in public places.

• *Distractibility.* The child has trouble concentrating and doesn't seem to "listen." This is common enough with young children, but here it's a question of degree. The child may be unable to concentrate for even a brief period of time. He is forgetful and disorganized.

• *Negative persistence and poor adaptability.* This is a stubborn, strong-willed child, with very definite preferences. Once used to things she doesn't like change. She seems rigid and gets "locked in"; the child also has trouble changing activities (for instance, she won't leave the house for the playground but then won't go home without a scene); and when she wants something, she goes on nagging or whining if she doesn't get it. She can be very particular if things aren't just right.

This kind of refusal to give up and inability to move on has a positive side. A highly persistent child is able to stay for a long time with an activity she likes, such as Lego or puzzles, or a favorite TV program (which the child may want repeated every day for weeks). This is a real blessing for parents. It also explains something that parents are often puzzled by: high distractibility (when he doesn't like an activity) co-existing with high persistence, positive or negative (when he really likes or wants something).

• *Initial withdrawal.* The first response of the child to strangers, new places, new baby-sitters, is to withdraw; the characteristic behavior is to cling and refuse to talk. She may get upset, even tantrum. Sometimes she may reject new clothes, foods, or experiences.

• *High intensity.* This is evident as loudness in laughing, crying, and excitement. The house is never quiet.

• *Irregularity.* Feeding and sleeping problems from infancy continue, but now the battle over bedtime becomes prominent; specific sleeptimes cannot be imposed on the child because he isn't always tired at the same time; awakening during the night may occur, and the child is frequently in the parents' bed. Irregular appetite seems more like willfulness. Toilet training can be hard because of irregular bowel habits. His moods can change suddenly and unpredictably.

• *Low sensory threshold.* Power struggles or tantrums occur over clothes that "don't feel right," shoelaces have to be retied endlessly, tags in clothing have to be removed; excess sensitivity may be evident to noises, lights, or smells; the child notices minor changes in food taste or appearance. She refuses to wear a coat in the middle of winter, complaining she is too hot; or she will wear only underwear in the home. She is easily overstimulated in crowded places. She is also a very aware child, often creative, with unusual and interesting preferences.

• *Negative mood.* The child's basic mood is serious, sullen, or cranky; he does not express pleasure openly; he seems to be an unhappy child.

In general the mothers of difficult 2- and 3-year-olds describe them as stubborn and contrary. Power struggles are common and loud, long temper tantrums often occur. Parents are frequently embarrassed by the child in public places.

Children 4 to 6 Years

Parents expect that by age 4 a child will become somewhat easier. But the difficult child is becoming harder
and harder to manage. The vicious circle may be fully
evident in the family, and the child is often suffering
wear and tear. He may become whiny, complaining,
nagging, and demand ever-increasing attention. Self-
image problems are starting to surface.

The child's entry into nursery school brings new
anxiety for the parents of certain kinds of difficult children. The highly active, distractible child has trouble
sitting still, paying attention, and standing on line. His
impulsiveness and poor control cause problems with teachers and with other children. Poorly adaptable children
have difficulty with sharing and with changing activities, while children who withdraw initially stand on the
periphery and won't join in. The low-threshold child may
dress in the same clothes day after day or wear "funny,"
inappropriate outfits that mark him as "different." Some
difficult children, however, improve as they begin nursery school if this is a positive experience for them; they
may be considerably easier to manage at school than
they are at home.

HOW DO THESE TEMPERAMENTAL QUALITIES INTERACT?

Difficult children are usually difficult in more than one
temperamental area, and these traits interlock. Let's
look at an example of how three areas of temperament
can interplay in reaction to a new article of clothing.

The mother is very excited; she's just found a pair of
jeans in her daughter's favorite color, lavender. She brings
this present home and gives it to her little girl, thinking
that this gift will, at last, please her child, who is very
fussy about what she wears. The little girl's first reaction is, "I don't like them!" (*initial withdrawal*). Her
mother is surprised and unhappy but decides not to force
her daughter to take the gift, so she leaves the jeans in
her daughter's room and goes to the kitchen. After nearly

an hour passes, her daughter emerges from her room to announce to her mother that the new jeans are quite nice after all, it's just that she doesn't want to take off what she's wearing to try them on. "Mommy, I really like these new jeans." "Then why don't we try them on?" her mother suggests. "Because I like my own pants better. I'm not used to the new ones," the child says (*poor adaptability*). At the end of the day, the little girl has finally made up her mind to remove her own worn pants and try on the new ones. Her mother is excited. The child likes the gift. She helps her daughter put on the new jeans and pull up the zipper. Immediately the child makes a face. "They don't feel good. I hate them. They're too stiff. I want to take them off" (*low sensory threshold*).

The little girl in this example withdraws from new situations; is poorly adaptable; and has a low sensory threshold, which makes her quite sensitive to how things feel. The jeans are *new,* which is the first problem. When the child gets used to them, she is unable to adapt easily to the thought of *changing* her pants; when she finally does change, the jeans are *stiff* and *pressed* and *starched,* in contrast to her own nice, soft worn clothes. The reactions of such a child might be similar if you offered her a new food instead of what she was used to, or if you took her to a new place. In more extreme cases, this interaction of temperamental features can create many tense situations, with the child increasingly upset due to the interplay of reactions, and the parent angry and feeling inadequate because she feels thwarted at every turn. It always helps to know that *there are reasons* for these behaviors.

Parents need to look for the underlying temperamental causes when confronting their child's difficult behavior. Remember that behavior can often be linked to a difficult trait, or to an interplay of difficult traits. Let's look at one behavior, a tantrum, to try to see what the underlying causes might be.

A mother buys an ice cream cone for her child on a very hot day. It's the child's favorite flavor, mint chocolate chip. The mother pays for the ice cream and takes the child, carrying the cone, outside to sit on a bench in front of the store. The child begins to lick the ice cream eagerly, then notices that the ice cream has begun to melt, run down the cone, and drip onto her hand. With a shriek, the child throws the cone on the ground and starts to scream and cry, throwing a tantrum.

Another child cuts a finger and it starts to bleed, ever so slightly. Her immediate response is to cry hysterically, but even after the finger is fine, the crying and tantruming continue, for as long as an hour.

A third child wants a particular car for his birthday, one with doors and a trunk that open. His present from his parents is a more expensive car, but only the doors open; the trunk does not. The child tries to pry open the trunk, cannot, and has a tantrum.

In these three cases, all the children are easily upset and sensitive (*negative mood* and *low sensory threshold* play a role), but the trait that can be linked to the tantrums is *poor adaptability*. These children have little ability to adapt to the unexpected. The melting ice cream, the cut finger, and the alternate car model throw them off their balance. The resulting tantrums go on a long time because just as they get locked into a pleasurable activity, so they get locked into their unpleasant reactions. The result? The tantrum can seem endless.

IS MY CHILD REALLY "DIFFICULT"?

The primary way to judge whether your child is *temperamentally* difficult is to ask yourself whether his behaviors were present from an early age. As you have seen, temperament manifests itself early and is *part* of the child rather than a response to something outside him. Therefore, your child is not temperamentally difficult if:

• he *becomes* difficult at ages 24 to 30 months; perhaps he is entering the "terrible twos."

• his behavior problems have developed recently in *response* to events such as separation or divorce, birth of a new sibling, a move to another town or state, the onset of illness, or school and peer problems.

• his behavior is the result of a clear disorder
that can be diagnosed by a professional; this can
include autism, in which the child does not relate to
other people and has severe delay in language development; brain damage evident from birth or the
result of trauma or illness; or any other severe physical or mental disorder that not only will be evident
to most parents but also should be picked up early
by a pediatrician.

A special word about retarded children: A retarded
child falls below a certain level on tested measures of
intelligence. However, even if retarded, the child is still
an individual, with his own unique temperament. And if
he is temperamentally difficult, he, like any other child,
will benefit from improved management.

"HYPERACTIVITY"

Some of you may have been told that your child is
hyperactive. Chapter 4 focuses on this problem, but I
want to point out here that "hyperactive" has become a
buzz word that has lost much of its meaning. On the
continuum of behavior represented by activity level, as
with all temperamental traits, an easy-to-difficult range
exists. At one end is the low active child, at the other
the extremely active child. Somewhere along the spectrum, depending on whose opinion it is, a given child
may be "diagnosed." Parents should know that there
is no such thing as an objective test for hyperactivity
and that all so-called hyperactive children are also difficult in other areas of temperament, not just activity
level.

But whether you call them difficult children with a
very high activity level or "hyperactive," the principles
and techniques for dealing with them are the same as
for all difficult children. Some of these children have
other problems, such as language delays, motor problems, or early evidence of possible learning disabilities.
Here further evaluation is warranted, and special attention may be needed in these areas, but the principles of

understanding and managing their *behavior* are the same
for them as for other difficult children.

THE PARENTS OF THE DIFFICULT CHILD

Parents of children with only a few difficult traits usually feel somewhat bewildered, and though they usually
are coping, they don't feel that they're doing too well.
The parents of more difficult children are more confused
and feel guilty, angry, and inadequate. Parents of very
difficult or impossible "mother-killers" are, in addition,
often exhausted, depressed, embattled, and in trouble in
their marriages.

How has *your* life been changed by the presence of
this child? What are *your* feelings? The more difficult
the child, the more likely you are to find yourself caught
up in the vicious circle and the ripple effect, with your
child's behavior having an impact on your life both inside and outside your home. How often have you felt
guilty or inadequate as a parent? How often have you
been embarrassed by your child? How often, if you have
a really difficult child, have you felt alone?

Remember that you are not alone. There are three
to four million children in the United States who are
difficult and many more with difficult features. Their
parents feel much the way you do. They need to know
what they can do for their child and themselves. This
book will help you, and many of them as well, to manage
your difficult child, to make your home life better, to
make sure your young child won't develop emotional
problems, and to safeguard your marriage and your family as a whole. And you will do this by learning how to
understand your child and alter your approach to him.

My belief in the individuality of children is, as you
will see, a constant theme in this book. The difficult
child should be respected for the person he is. At the
same time the values and standards of your home are up
to you, the parents. I hope that I will help you strike a
balance between the two.

Once again, the child's temperament is not your

fault; with knowledge and understanding you'll become an expert on your child and his behavior; with that expertise, you'll reassert your role as leader and parent. This will give your child a real chance to realize his potential. You'd be surprised to know how many interesting, delightful, creative older children were once "difficult," too.

2

MOTHERS UNDER SIEGE

The strongest impression conveyed by mothers of really difficult children is that of parents who are not coping. These mothers are on the front line every day, and it is they who suffer the most. They feel they have no control over their children or, for that matter, over their own lives. When you see the mother dealing with such a child during one of the "bad" times, you feel as if you're watching two children engaged in a power struggle.

"I cannot make him listen," the mothers say. "I don't know how to handle her." "He's overwhelming." "We're at our wit's end." "I can't take him anymore." "I lose my temper all the time." "She drives me crazy."

In one extreme case, a mother consulted me on the eve of signing papers to relinquish her child for adoption. She felt she could no longer live with the stress that was ruining her life, her marriage, and her relationship with her other child. Her pain is almost unimaginable, yet the inability to impose effective discipline and the repeated power struggles that result can take a toll even on mothers of less difficult children. To learn how to break these patterns, you must understand how they come about.

THE CONCEPT OF FIT

Child mental health professionals often talk about the parent-child relationship in terms of "goodness of fit." Fit refers to how well the child and his environment match each other, particularly the child and his family, and most particularly the child and the primary caretaker—usually the mother. A difficult temperament should never be looked at in isolation. The question is always "How difficult is *this* child to his *particular* mother or family?" With a relatively easy child in an essentially normal family, good fit usually occurs naturally. And it is something that strongly affects the child's development.

There are two types of fit: emotional and behavioral. A good *emotional* fit means that the mother likes the child and that she feels comfortable with him. You can find cases of good emotional fit where the mother is low-key and has a high-strung child but she enjoys the child's *personality*. This is true in the case of one difficult little girl's mother who was exasperated by her child's often impossible behavior but who liked her child's funny and dramatic side, and found her keen interest in clothes and fashions something she could share and enjoy. The child's personality, as distinct from her temperament, was appealing to the mother, who was also very fashion-conscious.

Emotional fit can be understood by looking at the difference between liking and loving a child. Almost all parents love their children, but not all *like* them. A difficult child's likability will enable that child to have a good emotional fit with his mother. If you dislike your difficult child, your job as parent becomes even tougher. Negative mood and poor adaptability in particular are easy to dislike. The toughest behavior can be made more acceptable if the child is basically outgoing and positive.

Then there is *behavioral* fit: how acceptable is a child's behavior to his parents? An overactive child will fit much more easily into a casual home than a home in which strict standards are demanded. If the parents insist that all their precious collectibles and knickknacks be displayed, and they want their active child to learn not to touch them, there's going to be a good deal of conflict that might be avoided if the parents realistically acknowledged that it might be better to pack some things away and to cover their better furniture. An overactive, enthusiastic child would do better with a family whose standards were relaxed and who were more flexible about their life-style. Thus, when the child's environment is in general accord with him, you have a good behavioral fit. In general the more difficult the child's temperament, the more vulnerable he or she becomes to a poor emotional and/or behavioral fit.

We also have to ask what kind of person the mother is, for this can affect fit as well. A calmer, more phlegmatic mother who is not terribly excitable might be more objective in dealing with her child's behavior, although with a really difficult child, the patience of even the calmest mother can be stretched to its limits.

Improving the parent-child fit is perhaps the most important goal in my work with families.

"GOOD-ENOUGH" PARENTING

Mental health professionals also speak of the "good-enough parent." In most cases, this concept can be very reassuring. In effect, it means that you do *not* have to be a superparent to provide the environment your child needs to develop well. Good-enough parenting evolves naturally from the parent-child relationship, in which you and your child are both full-fledged partners. Every child teaches his mother how to parent by experience. Daily interaction is a learning process for both of you. As you learn, you become more self-confident and competent; your child helps you to become a good-enough parent.

All parents have expectations. These are shaped by their backgrounds, other parents' experiences, by movies and TV, by advertisements, and by books written to guide new mothers and fathers. No one imagines he will undergo a complete reversal of expectations. And when this occurs right from the start, the parents begin to feel embattled very early. As the days pass, you feel less self-confident and competent, and you fail to get the reinforcement that things are going right. And with the difficult child, good-enough parenting may not be enough to help the child; you do need to be a *better* than good-enough parent. This does not mean that you need to be more loving and caring, but you do need more understanding and more awareness of your child's unique needs.

And since the child's behavior often can be baffling, more understanding will help you deal with him. Again, I do not mean for you to prove you adore your child; in fact, it is a common mistake for parents to shower a difficult child with gifts to "make him happy." Extra love isn't enough, especially if it spoils the child. You need expertise!

POWER STRUGGLES AND THE VICIOUS CIRCLE

The difficult child's behavior creates a vicious circle of negative parent-child interaction. The extent of this depends on the degree of difficulty and the quality of the fit. Temperamental difficulties cause problem behavior in young children. Parents try to cope conventionally with these problems, but they get poor results. Discipline becomes more and more ineffective. There are constant power struggles between parent and child, during which the parent descends to the child's level, screaming when the child screams, throwing parental versions of the child's temper tantrums. The child, no longer perceiving the parent as an authority figure, becomes more resistant to the parent's demands and more locked into his own difficult behavior. The parent now varies discipline widely, totally at sea as to what to do, and fears, guilt, and anxieties begin to play a large role in the relationship with the child.

By now the parent and child are well into the vicious circle. The child is more likely to be clingy and fearful. He may have nightmares, appear oversensitive and cry easily, or even start saying things like "I'm bad." This makes the mother more anxious, guilty, and overinvolved with the child, and as she gets increasingly angry and frustrated, the child misbehaves more and the self-image problem worsens. If this keeps up over a number of years, the result can be psychiatric disorder for the child and untold strain, anguish, and trouble for both parents and their marriage.

The vicious circle can start early. In infancy, one of the central temperament issues is irregularity. The mother cannot "cue in" to the child, meaning that the baby isn't giving out predictable indicators of what he needs. The cues are erratic and are not picked up by the mother. And this is not because she's a bad mother; no one could pick up these cues. The baby cries when he's changed, not satisfied with being dry and powdered. And he cries after his nap, when he's rested, and after he's fed, when he's full. What's wrong? You can't tell when he's hungry and when he's not; you can't establish any patterns.

Such a baby screams a great deal and doesn't sleep for any regular period. The mother tries to soothe the child and is unsuccessful. The pediatrician says it's colic, but after several months the colic doesn't go away. The behavior continues, the mother gets more tired and angry. The father, if he shares any responsibilities for taking care of the child, is under pressure as well, and out of this anger and tiredness come patterns of blame.

As time goes on, parents in general and mothers in particular ask Why? Why? Why? How have we caused it? How are we responsible? The child's doctor says there's nothing wrong with him, so the implication is there's something wrong with *you*. Mothers find themselves wishing the child would throw a major tantrum in the doctor's office, so that he can see what they are talking about. And if you turn to other parents, no one understands what you're talking about, because they try to fit these behaviors into an understandable frame of reference. The child cries? Then he must be wet, hungry, sleepy, sick. But this child is *not* understandable. And their responses are only further confirmation that it must be something you're doing. After all, you've got this normal child, and all other parents can raise their normal children, but you can't. Therefore there must be something wrong with you.

It *is* much harder with a difficult child.

WHY IS HE DOING THIS TO ME?

As the child gets older, parents begin to ascribe motives to his behavior. I often hear parents say, "He's doing this on purpose," the implication being that the parent

feels, "The child is out to get me." The little boy who
doesn't smile when his father buys him a present, the
little girl who isn't hungry for her favorite dinner spe-
cially prepared by her tired mother, the child who screams
and cries when taken to the circus for the first time—
these are children who may be behaving a certain way
because their temperaments dictate their actions. But
their angry, disappointed parents who have tried so hard
to please them don't see it that way. They think their
children are *intentionally* thwarting them. The messages
the child is giving out are ambiguous; there seems to be
no reason for the child's behavior. The parent then looks
for motives in an effort to understand what is going on.
Often this leads to a descent to the child's level, to
feeling victimized, exhausted, and incapable of coping. It
is obviously nearly impossible to have a good fit with a
child if you feel he is out to "get" you. Experienced
parents are less likely to assign blame since they may
have had success with their previous child and may not
feel as guilty.

INEFFECTIVE DISCIPLINE

Ascribing motives to the child can lead the parents to
punish for motivation rather than for behavior. For example, it is unfair to punish the child with irregular
rhythms for not being hungry at dinner. He may in fact
not be hungry at dinner*time*. But the mother who per-
ceives this as a slap in the face—"he's just doing this to
get back at me because he saw me slaving in the kitchen
for two hours"—is angrily going to send the child to his
room.

A mother of an extremely active child may get un-
nerved by all of his running around; he may, in fact,
have broken something as he dashes pell-mell around
the house. But to punish him by making him sit in a
corner is punishing him for his nature. Such behavior
should be restrained and managed, not punished.

The problem is that difficult children *provoke* ineffective discipline. Their behavior is often bewildering to
the parents, who then become more and more tentative

in their response. From this follow inconsistency, negotiation, bribery, and overreaction.

This contrasts sharply with the components of good discipline, which include consistency, understanding what's happening and what you're doing, clear and brief responses exerted with a full sense of authority and administered calmly.

"I feel I'm constantly battling the child"

Ineffective discipline has a wearing effect on the mother and child that can prove destructive in the long run. With an extremely difficult child and an embattled, exhausted mother, the day-to-day aspects of life begin to form into a series of continuing power struggles. Eventually there can be fights over *all* the child's behavior, from morning until night, encompassing everything from clothing to food to playtime to school. It seems as if nothing will ever be simple again.

Of course, the degree of difficulty affects how the mother responds; the more difficult the child, the more the mother is affected. The experience of the parent counts, for those less experienced do have a harder time. The personality and temperament of the parents come into play, as do issues of family life such as job stability, health, the well-being of the marriage, and financial security. These can all influence how deeply affected the parents will be by their child.

The constant battling arises for the most part from *an established habit pattern between the child and the mother*. Not only is the child repeatedly misbehaving; it is very important for the mother to realize that *her* ineffective response has also become habitual, and is in fact *reinforcing* the bad behavior. The parent wants the child to do something and the child won't; or the child misbehaves and the parent wants to punish him. The child won't listen to the parent; the parent gets furious: "You don't respect me," "You want to make me mad," "You know how I hate it when you won't answer me." The parent and the child get locked in, escalate, and battling ensues.

This interaction is repeated in a variety of everyday settings: A 6-year-old boy calls his mother names. "You're a dope," he says. "You're stupid." This infuriates his mother, who goes crazy as soon as she hears this. She screams, "How dare you say this to me" to her child and sends him to his room, slamming the door behind him. Every time he calls her a name she reacts the same way. And each time she dares him to, he calls her a name again. *Both* mother and child are locked into this pattern.

The mother of a difficult 3-year-old dreads taking her into stores. One day she has to go to a bakery to pick up a cake for her husband's birthday party that evening. As soon as her daughter enters the shop with her mother, she gets cranky and whiny. As they wait for the cake, the child's fussing grows worse. The mother says, "You can have a cookie. Pick something out!" The child points to a huge cookie shaped like a teddy bear. The mother tells the clerk to pick it out of the selection under the counter. Then the child points to a large cookie shaped like a train. "This one, too," she says. Her mother says no, she may have only one. But the child gets locked into the idea of having both. "Train, train, train!" she screams. Her mother shouts, "No!" The child cries. The mother yells, "Choose, choose, pick *one!*" In the end, the mother has to drag the screaming child from the bakery, in the process leaving behind the cake she had come to buy. "Why does this happen every time I take her to a store?" she asks herself. Yet another example of a negative repetitive habit pattern.

When the issue of sleeptime is raised in the house of a child whose rhythms are irregular, there is trouble. Usually the sleep problems are longstanding, so that by age 3 or 4 the ritual bedtime battles are strongly established in the family. If the child isn't tired at the same time, he'll come to fight bedtime. He'll start to appear in the doorway, asking for juice, a story, his mommy, or a favorite toy. These appearances will happen more and more frequently, and as the parent tries to force the child to close his eyes and sleep, the child will begin to get anxious and fearful about going to bed because he

knows there will be a struggle, and he will get even
more set in his resistance to sleep. Finally, the scene
will end in tears and guilt. The parent, feeling com-
pletely ineffectual, begins to feel sorry for this poor,
woebegone child. And a clever child may come to exploit
that pity.

The issues can be many with difficult children, ranging from food to sleep to clothing to toys to school to
playtime, but when they are linked by this constant
struggling, the effect on the parents is the same. Poor
fit, ineffective authority and discipline, the assigning of
motivations, the lack of control, the day-to-day power
struggles all contribute to the vicious circle. The feeling
of being under siege comes to define the whole range of
responses elicited by the parents' relationship with their
very difficult child.

WHAT HAPPENS TO THE MOTHER?

The primary caretaker, most commonly the mother, finds
herself responding to this embattled situation in a variety of ways. Not all mothers have all these responses. I
am presenting a deliberately bleak picture. There are
many mitigating factors, including the child, who may
be interesting and even fun to be with. But in general,
the mother's most common responses include:

Bewilderment: This is the mother who says, "I don't
know where he's coming from." She simply does not
understand what her child is doing, and she cannot
build any consistent responses to him. Her responses
change along with the child's behavior. For example, the
child is looking forward to going to a birthday party.
The party comes, and the child goes off happily. A week
later, the circumstances seem to be the same, another
birthday party, but this time the child has a temper
tantrum. The mother is not going to know why, and this
is going to upset her. Expectations can play a big role in
contributing to parental bewilderment. An extremely
fashion-conscious mother will have a lot of trouble understanding a child who wants to wear the same cloth-

ing day after day. A quiet, shy parent will be far more
affected by a very loud, high-intensity child.

Exhaustion: Some of these children need constant
management, and parenting them is simply hard work.
First of all, you may start out more exhausted following
an infancy in which your sleep was severely limited by
feeding and sleep problems. Second, you may be over-
managing your child doing a lot of chasing, cleaning
up, preparing special meals, giving the child constant
attention without any resulting change in the child's
behavior. This is certainly exhausting. One mother prepared a separate, special dinner for her difficult little
girl, serving it at 4:00 P.M. each night, because she said
that's when her daughter liked to eat. "She's used to it
then," the mother said. "I can't change." She then had to
serve the rest of the family, two other children and her
husband and herself, at 6:30 P.M. This kind of thing only
increases the burden on a mother already strained by
the battles and strong emotions which are typical of an
established vicious circle.

Anger: Mothers who aren't coping well with their
difficult children are usually angry. A lot of anger comes
out in their ineffective discipline, a great deal of shouting and sometimes hitting, which doesn't do much good.
The mother has fantasies of getting rid of her child, of
running away, or of giving the child away. Anger is
expressed not only at the child but also at the husband
and at the child's siblings. During one of the many
power struggles it may result in loss of control and,
sadly, excessive physical punishment.

Guilt: As a direct result of the mother's feeling of
ineffectiveness, there is an increased feeling of guilt, of
being the cause of the child's problems. This comes on
top of the things that are said to the parent by doctors,
teachers, other mothers, her husband, her own family, or
her in-laws. Guilt results in constant self-questioning,
tentativeness, and anxiety. A mother who feels this way
believes that the world thinks she's a rotten mother and

that her child is a rotten kid from a rotten home, and this makes the mother feel helpless. The mother in the park *assumes* that everyone blames her when her overstimulated child lashes out at other children there. A mother who severely reprimands her child in front of his grandmother may elicit the response, "What are you doing to him? Why can't you handle him better? Did I do that to you when you were a child?" She already *knows* her mother thinks it's all her fault.

Embarrassment: All parents know this feeling, but for the parent of a difficult child it is multiplied a thousandfold. This is an external feeling, as guilt is an internal one, and occurs most often in public places when mothers notice the stares of other mothers, store clerks, shoppers, waiters, librarians, bus drivers, and other witnesses to the child's misbehavior—and, more pointedly, to their own inability to control the child.

Inadequacy: The mother feels ineffective and helpless because she can't control the child. Comparing herself with other mothers or with her own mother only makes it worse. A mother who brings her child to a recreational program is in a group with a dozen other mothers and children. Mothers in these situations watch each other and compare their children's behavior. But a difficult child who has trouble switching activities can rivet the attention of everyone in the group. When the teacher asks that the children put away their smocks and put down their paintbrushes, the difficult child may object strongly. Change may be hard for him to undergo in such a short time, and misbehavior may follow, including a possible tantrum. By the time the poor mother has her child out of the smock and away from the easel, the other children have taken off their sneakers and socks to participate in gymnastics on the mats. And the mother has to battle the child to get him to take off his shoes. With all eyes on her recalcitrant child, how could she possibly feel competent?

Depression: Most mothers of difficult children feel depressed at times, particularly after a very bad day or week. Occasionally, if there is a hereditary predisposition or if other aspects of her environment are also very stressful, a mother may develop clinical depression. This is not just a passing low mood, but rather a syndrome that has other symptoms associated with it: appetite and sleep problems, loss of concentration, low energy level, constant self-critical thoughts, and a pessimistic view of the future. Clinical depression can be treated, and anyone experiencing these symptoms should seek further help.

Isolation: Many mothers feel shunned by other parents who don't want their children playing with the "difficult" one. This happens particularly if the child is active, gets overstimulated, and lashes out at other children. If the family lives in a small community the mother can feel totally alone; she thinks that no one knows what's happening to her or has any understanding of her dilemma. Worse, she thinks she is the only mother who has ever experienced this problem. She may look for answers in books on child-rearing or try to speak with the pediatrician, but no one seems to understand *her* dilemma.

Victimization: This is perhaps the most pervasive response among really embattled mothers. "Why is he doing this to me?" "He hates me." "He's doing this on purpose." "He really wants to make me mad." As mothers lose the sense of being effective, their child suddenly seems to be the powerful one in the relationship. He controls how you feel; he controls what your day is like, good or bad; he is in control of your life. You have become his victim.

Lack of satisfaction: You feel that you're carrying an immense burden, that being a mother is so much more difficult for you than it is for anyone else, and yet you have so little return for your efforts. You work harder doing the simplest things, such as dressing your child or preparing his food; you need hours to do what it takes other mothers minutes to accomplish; your pres-

ence is required virtually constantly. But many of the
small (or even large) satisfactions of parenthood escape
you. For all that effort, there should be more to show,
and there isn't.

Feeling trapped: Mothers of difficult children feel as
if they're unable to change their fate. They're stuck with
a child who is unresponsive and hard to raise; they
think that no one understands what they're going through,
and the burden falls on them. Many of these women—
far more than you'd imagine—have strong fantasies of
running away from their homes and from their difficult
children.

Over-involvement: This is extremely common in mothers of difficult children, a mix of many different feelings.
Paradoxically, in view of all the other feelings, you become very, very involved in your child's difficulties and
overprotective of his needs. This stems from a feeling
that only you, as his mother, can understand what he's
going through, and your perception of his suffering
stimulates your need to hover over him. Such overpro-
tectiveness may relate to a mother's own conflicts about
being a mother. For example, these feelings will be exaggerated in a woman who was inappropriately expected
to be very independent and grown up when she was a
child. For her, the need to protect her own child will be
exaggerated.

All of this, combined with what your child is doing
every day, contributes to the feeling that you, the parent, are under siege and that the enemy is your own
child. The way to resolve this unhappy situation and to
interrupt the chain reaction of events in the vicious
circle is to learn everything you can about why your
child behaves the way he does, and then to put into
practice the techniques for management and adult authority that you will be learning. By understanding how
to parent these children effectively, you will you be able
to escape some of the painful and potentially harmful
consequences both for the child and yourself.

3

THE RIPPLE EFFECT

The impact of the difficult child on his world can be likened to throwing a stone into a quiet pond. The first splash, the greatest impact, is the child's interaction with the mother. But that stone also creates concentric ripples that spread outward until virtually the entire pond is disturbed. The child's temperament and behavior affect his relationship with every member of his family. Some children's behavior can also affect peers, teachers, caretakers, baby-sitters, or other adults.

The world also affects your child. Development is a continuous process of interaction between the child and his environment, and as your child grows, temperament becomes less important in determining his behavior. His personality is increasingly a product not only of his temperament, but also of his character which includes his attitudes, motivations, and the impact on him of the people, places, and things he sees and comes to know.

It's never the child in isolation, but rather the child in the family and in the world.

In this chapter I ask you to look at this ripple effect. We'll start with those closer, more intense circles and work outward. Let us begin with your own marriage.

THE FATHER AND THE MARRIAGE

It's obvious by now how the mother and the difficult child can become locked into a vicious circle. The father's role, unless he is the primary caretaker, is somewhat different. Because he is around less, his relationship with the child usually is less intense and therefore easier. The marriage, however, is often affected to a greater or lesser extent, depending on how difficult the child is and whether other marital problems exist.

I commonly see four types of reaction:

The father may feel shut out. The complexity and intensity of some of these mother-child relationships make fathers feel ignored and not a full member of the family. When a father remains home on the weekend, for instance, he will be witness to some of the continuing struggles between the mother and the child, such as over getting dressed in the morning. The long, drawn-out procedures that may be involved require a great deal of time and the total participation of the mother. The father often finds that he can neither interfere nor contribute. The same applies to any other areas in which the child's behavior has elicited such a complicated response from the mother. "Where am *I* in all this?" the father asks himself.

The father questions what the mother is doing. It's not hard to imagine why a father would also ask, "Is this all really necessary? Couldn't you just *make* him put on his clothes, with no fussing?" Because he may not have been around to witness the full development of these patterns involving mother and child, he may question their value. In fact, one father who didn't understand why his wife spent so much time dressing their daughter in the morning and doing her hair volunteered to take over for his wife one morning, convinced *he* could do it faster. After two hours of cajoling, shouting, and hysteria (and the tantruming was shared by child *and* father), he returned, chastened, to his wife, to say that he really hadn't understood what was going on before. Now he did. Questioning of the mother's approach, however, can be as simple and devastating as a father returning home at night to a screaming child, a burned dinner, and a sullen older sibling, to say to his exhausted, angry wife, "What is the matter with you? Can't you handle this kid? What are you doing that makes it so hard?" Out of these situations come patterns of blame, an undermining of the support system between husband and wife, and eventually marital discord.

The mother has no energy for the father. After a day in which she has spent perhaps four hours soothing tantrums, unhappiness, crankiness, dissatisfaction with food, toys, or clothes (or all of them), another four hours trying to do housework, shopping, and laundry while still overseeing her exhausting child, followed by a crisis-filled dinner and bedtime drama, she wants a few minutes to herself before she falls asleep. She has almost nothing left over for her husband, and so there is less sex, less closeness, and almost no time together as a couple.

The mother can become jealous of the father's relatively conflict-free relationship with the child. Because the mother is with the child all day, there is plenty of time for their responses to get established and locked in: the power struggles intensify as each day passes. (This explains why it's always the *primary caretaker* who has the most trouble with a young difficult child, a fact that is a source of guilt for many mothers.) But the father, who is home far less, often is not present for many of these episodes, so his relationship may be easier. After one of these classically awful days with the child, the mother may not appreciate a father who comes in to her and says, "Gee, honey, he's really OK with me. I don't understand why you had such a bad time of it today." And, indeed, the child can be easier with the father. This does not sit well with the mother.

The main result of these problems seems to be the lack of support, the feeling of many wives that their husbands are not *behind* them or sympathetic to them in their plight.

Interestingly enough, many mothers have mixed feelings of anger and protectiveness toward their difficult child. On the one hand, the mothers feel wrung out by the child and that they have nothing to give to the marriage anymore. Yet when their husbands get angry and attack the child as the cause of many of their marital difficulties, the mothers get very defensive and immediately protect the child. Thus, if the marriage was strained before the birth of the child, that situation will only worsen. A child like this can split a fragile but holding marriage wide open.

SIBLINGS

Imagine how hard it can be for the siblings of a really difficult child. They are often resentful of all the attention the difficult child receives, and they may feel neglected and "left out" of the family as well. Many siblings express a great deal of worry about the problem child, concerned over all the crying and negative behavior. To get their fair share of attention, some siblings may begin to misbehave, while others become model children. Problems with the "goody two-shoes" child can surface later.

The parents of a difficult child will often raise their expectations for the sibling and ask more of the older child in terms of independence and maturity. I have frequently heard mothers talk about the easier child as "my big boy" or "the really mature one in the family," only to discover that the mother is referring to a child of 5 or 6. Conversely, parents talk about the difficult child as if he were a very small baby, or toddler, when he may be 7 or 8.

CHILD-FAMILY INTERACTION: HOW IT LOOKS IN REAL LIFE

Let us now see how the interaction between a very difficult child and her family works in a real-life situation, a family dinner. You will see how the temperamental features of a small girl aged 4 cause problems for her mother, her father, and her older sister.

This is a family in which dinner is normally served at the same time each night, 6:30 P.M. The parents like to enjoy a full meal, with a first course; a serving of meat, potatoes, and vegetables to follow; then a cup of coffee and occasionally dessert. Normally the table is set in the dining room and the family is called in to dinner by the mother.

Because the difficult child has *irregular rhythms,* she isn't hungry each night at six-thirty, and this night is no exception. She does not want to stop watching TV and come to the table to eat because she isn't interested in food and because she has gotten involved watching a TV show. Due to *poor adaptability,* she can't easily handle the transition from what she really likes doing.

The father believes that the mother's efforts to control the child are not firm enough, so he regularly intervenes and there is an exchange of criticism from father to mother over the handling of the child. "Be firm," the father counsels, shaking his finger at his wife. "Let her know you mean business. You never sound like you're really going to *do* anything," he adds as the mother tries to pry the child from the TV. She is unsuccessful and finally, with a huge sigh, the father has to rise from his chair and go inside to fetch the child. But his threats get no results, so he clicks off the TV, causing the child to scream, and to get her to stop screaming, he spanks her. Then he drags her to the dinner table and forcibly puts her into her chair. She is cranky, disagreeable, tear-stained, and ready to cry in a second, an exaggeration of her normal *mood,* which is *negative.* Her older sister makes a face at her that the mother sees, and is sharply rebuked.

Soup is served and everyone starts to eat, except the little girl, who is squirming in her chair, knocking her silverware together, and kicking the leg of the table. She cannot ordinarily sit still because she has a *high activity level.* She also will not touch soup of any kind because it always tastes "too hot" (she is quite sensitive to food temperature because she has a *low sensory threshold*). The main course is meat loaf, a food the little girl normally enjoys, but this night she says it smells "funny" and she won't touch it (*low sensory threshold* again). Her mother had run out of the tomato sauce she normally uses and substituted a jarred spaghetti sauce, and the child will not eat because she has picked up the different taste. She starts to tantrum when her parents insist she try to eat some meat loaf. Her father tries to control her, her mother gets upset because she sees the dinner hour

ruined again, the older sister can't stand her father's
yelling, and the difficult child is getting even more locked
into her negative responses. The battle lines are being
firmly drawn.

You can easily see that the child does not "fit" too
well with her family. For one thing, her parents are
trying to force the child into their patterns, while the
child has her own temperament with its own style. When
conflicts like this occur with very young children other
problems can follow. For example, a headstrong child,
boxed into a power struggle with her parents, will eventually refuse to eat even when she *is* hungry. Paradoxically, excessive criticism and negative attention *reinforce*
the "bad" behavior—a very important principle. The
child's fussiness over the smell and taste of food come
from a real sensitivity to them, but the outcry generated
simply exaggerates her response. Thus the negative interaction of the difficult child and her family results in
many ways from the chain reaction set up by her behavior. This reaction in turn reinforces the behavior. Not
understanding the underlying issues, parents simply don't
have the tools to deal with the child and to unlock these
destructive patterns.

OTHER PRESSURES ON THE PARENTS

Other things can affect a family and may be made worse
by the presence of a difficult child and, in turn, affect
the parents' handling of the child. These factors can
include:

Young marriages. The prognosis for a marriage when
a couple has married extremely young is generally more
questionable, and the problems of these couples can be
made far worse by the birth of a difficult child. Financial
problems, feelings of being trapped, loss of independence
before you've had a chance to "really live" can all be
intensified, and since the participants in the marriage
may not be fully mature, they will not cope as well as an
older, more experienced couple might.

Personal problems. Alcoholism that existed before a difficult child came into the family and that had been brought under control could flare up again after the child appears; if the husband has the drinking problem, frequently the support and interest as well as the love of his wife has helped him keep his problem under control. A difficult child makes it almost impossible for a wife to pay as much attention to her husband as before, and when he loses her support, he may fall off the wagon. Obviously, a drinking wife may want to go back to drinking under the stress of a hard-to-raise child.

A parent who has suffered previous episodes of depression or anxiety but who has recovered and has been functioning can relapse after the arrival of a difficult child. The stress may be too much to cope with. Conversely, personal and marital problems make adults less effective and secure in their parental role. If these problems are significant, make sure that you address them, and don't ascribe everything that goes on in your family to the child's difficult temperament.

In-law troubles. In some families there are acceptance problems for either spouse: their in-laws may not like or approve of them, thus causing cracks in the marriage as their support is withdrawn. A difficult child may bring more blame and criticism to the husband or wife already in disfavor with the in-laws (or with their own family, for that matter). And this can create real problems for the marriage, especially if the families live relatively close by.

Financial and job pressures. Money is one of the major issues in any marriage. When a difficult child adds the extra stress, the pressure may prove too great. On the husband's part, a man in a high-pressure job, someone who has to work very long hours or move his family from place to place, or simply worry a lot about his business future, needs a tranquil home atmosphere. This is clearly not possible in a family with a difficult child. And what about a working mother, particularly one in a demanding job? She finds herself "at work" seven days and nights a week.

The "Golden Couple." There are also problems for people who seem to have no problems at all. Think of the couple with everything, for whom life has always seemed exciting, fruitful, fulfilling, and most importantly, easy. Everything has fallen from the tree with just a few shakes—that is, until the birth of this child. A difficult child born into this kind of marriage can cause stress and divisiveness. The guilt, the blaming, and the intensity of the family's response can all be magnified by the sense that this has never happened to them before and that it has spoiled *everything*.

Expectations of motherhood. For the mother who wants to be the "perfect mother," and who invests a lot of her self-esteem in this, the difficult child can be extremely hard to handle not only behaviorally but also inwardly. The marriage inevitably suffers. Conversely, the insecure mother who has little confidence in her ability to be a "good" mother may be devastated by her "incompetence." Her lack of confidence and feelings of inadequacy will affect her role as a wife as well.

Of course, all of these problems could affect any marriage regardless of whether the child is difficult or not. But the presence of a difficult child will *aggravate* them to a greater degree than they might have been otherwise.

THE EXTENDED FAMILY

In the extended family, blame can get exaggerated. Normal concern for the well-being of the grandchild gets blown out of proportion in relation to the behavior of the child. "What are you doing wrong with him?" the grandparents say to their children. "When I raised you, this never happened. You must be doing this wrong." Frequently this impression is complicated by the fact that some difficult children will not behave as badly with their grandparents as they do with their parents. This deepens the patterns of blame. "He's so good with me," the grandmother says. "Don't yell at him. Don't be so hard on him." Feelings of inadequacy and guilt in response to parental criticism can be very strong for the parent of the difficult child. Conversely, grandparents find very active children particularly difficult because they have trouble looking after them. In both instances the normal system of support provided by grandparents can be eroded, and the loss can affect the family's well-being. Obviously, the more support systems a family has and the stronger they are, the better.

Assigning blame for the existence of the child can also occur among members of the extended family: "She's not like anyone on *our* side of the family" is a frequent comment. Often the mother and father are made to feel guilty for allowing these "bad genes" to emerge. And the mother, especially, feels she must question her behavior, diet, routine, and activities during pregnancy. What did *she* do wrong that might have caused this different—and unrecognizable—child to emerge?

Many adults continue to experience subtle conflicts with their own parents. The stress produced by a difficult child can exaggerate such conflicts and cause them to surface.

WORKING MOTHERS

In general, mothers of difficult children are fighting a lot of guilt, whether they are working mothers or not. And the mother who returns to work, the mother of any young child, invariably has some mixed feelings. These feelings then become quite exaggerated and may be very hard to handle for the mother of a young difficult child.

The main issue for the working mother is the quality of substitute care; a good fit with a housekeeper, baby-sitter, or day-care facility is very important. If the person you have chosen to care for your child is understanding and if you find her easy to communicate with, the situation is likely to work out well. A good caretaker may in fact be more accepting of your child. For example, a family day-care worker or regular baby-sitter may

be more relaxed about irregular mealtimes and sleeptimes, or may not mind a loud, very intense child, while
the child's mother is more bothered by these things. A
caretaker may simply have more energy and objectivity
each day to cope with all the problems. Your own feelings toward the child may be more positive when you
return home after a day away from the house.

Trouble begins, however, if jealousy arises between
the mother and the caregiver. The mother feels the
caregiver is taking over her role; the caregiver doesn't
want anyone to interfere with the way she is managing
things. Such problems can multiply greatly with a difficult child. A housekeeper may establish a way of handling the child that makes the mother jealous. After all,
if she (the mother) can't handle her own child, who can?
Why should someone else have an easier time of it? And
the housekeeper may resent it if she senses that her
authority with the child is being undermined. The mother
can wind up feeling as if she's competing with the
caregiver, while the caregiver may communicate some of
her resentment of the mother to the child. If the child
senses this division, his behavior can take a turn for
the worse.

Not all caretakers can cope with a really difficult
child, especially over a long period of time. If your caretaker is not a good substitute for you, if the only available day care cannot offer individual attention and
continuity to your young child, or if the child's behavior
is such that no substitute could handle him, you may
have to make the unhappy choice of giving up your job
for a while or postponing your return to work. This may
cause economic hardship, and it can make a mother
even more resentful of her "problem" child. But in some
cases it is the only solution.

DIVORCE AND ITS CONSEQUENCES

When there has been disagreement and fighting leading
up to the separation and the divorce, this conflict becomes an added factor in the vicious circle. A bitter
divorce is stressful for all children, but it is especially

hard on difficult children. The child's behavior will almost surely worsen during this period, and the guilt of the parents adds additional strain. On the other hand, I strongly believe that it is, in the long run, worse for the child if a couple that has clearly reached the end of the road continues in a tense and unhappy relationship "for the child's sake."

Other problems emerge during visitation. Because of the differences in approach in two different homes, the child may experience a certain amount of built-in inconsistency. Difficult children need consistency and routine more than most; when, unhappily, in some divorces, inconsistency is used deliberately by one parent to undermine the other, the difficult child becomes the victim.

Once divorced, the mother's responsibilities increase. The support that can be available in a good marriage is absent. And, clearly, the working single mother is not able to quit her job. She *must* find proper alternative care, or settle for what is available. Sheer fatigue may complicate her relations with her child; how well can you handle a tantrum after you've been at work for eight hours and still have to shop and prepare dinner? Single mothers often find that they have little time for themselves and can become quite resentful of the child. At the same time their relationship with the difficult child is usually very close, to the point of overinvolvement.

The remarriage of a parent brings another significant adult into the difficult child's life. Problems with inconsistency may arise again and need new solutions.

Well-meaning parents should inform themselves on the issues created for children by marital strife, divorce, single parenting, and step-families. When the child involved is temperamentally difficult, this extra dimension needs to be carefully considered as well.

THE ADOPTED DIFFICULT CHILD

There are certain issues built into the situation of adoption that become exaggerated when a difficult child is involved, just as the issues of the working mother and the single parent are. An adopted child is in a way a "genetic stranger" to his parents. The kind of intuitive understanding we often experience with our own children may be absent when the child is adopted. This is not necessarily negative. It can be easier knowing that this is not your child biologically, and thus much of the guilt surrounding genes, pregnancy, and birth is alleviated. "It's not coming from me," you think. "And it wasn't anything I did during my pregnancy." The search for reasons can lead to a blaming game in which each parent accuses the other of contributing to the child's problematic makeup. At least this is not present when the child is adopted.

But if there is any ambivalence attached to the adoption, this feeling will be exaggerated by the presence of the difficult child and may turn into a more rejecting attitude toward the child. Stronger feelings on the order of "He's not really mine" may emerge far more clearly. Another reaction I sometimes see is the tendency to explain any behavior, including that which is clearly temperamental in origin, as due to the psychological effects of the adoption. You can easily miss the point with your child if you have such an attitude.

PUBLIC PLACES

So often parents who feel they can somehow manage their children in their own home are thrown by contact with the outside world. Many parents bring to parenthood an exaggerated sense of their own responsibility, so that when their child misbehaves they feel too responsible. With the difficult child, the sensation that you are being looked at and *judged* results in embarrassment and shame.

Stores and supermarkets: These are places that are hard for the active, distractible, impulsive child who will want to run around and touch everything. This desire, combined with the overstimulation of the loud, busy, brightly lit store, can cause such a child to become wild. Even if the child is in a stroller or sitting in a shopping cart, there can be trouble; these kids may try to grab everything in sight. They are loud and vocal about the items they want to have. Tantrums can easily follow.

This contrasts with the reaction of a child who withdraws in new situations. If such a child is taken into a busy supermarket before he's ready, a tantrum may result for different reasons. If the child is generally uncomfortable with new situations, imagine what a supermarket looks like to him. First of all, there are the busy entrances, with people quickly pushing inside. Then there is the noise level, which is generally high, with people shouting about orders and deliveries, plus an overlay of piped-in, uptempo music. This scene is augmented by the bright lights and by the array of colors, textures, different packaging, and advertising signs. On a weekend, when the store is especially crowded, the people only add to this jumble of sensory stimuli. Combine all of this with the well-meaning interest of strangers who, seeing a confused, unhappy child, ask, "What's wrong?" or offer cookies or a piece of candy, and you may find your child clinging, crying, and eventually screaming.

Seeing the place through the child's eyes might help you to understand his plight, but what about yours? After all, your family has to have something to eat. So you try to soothe the child and then plunge ahead into the store. The resulting scene, with either a grabbing, distracted, overactive child or a cringing, withdrawn one, is extremely embarrassing. After all, here are lots of other mothers and fathers accompanied by relatively docile children, and yours is causing a highly visible scene. The child will, by this time, rebuff your attempts to calm him or to offer some goodies to quiet him down. And you will feel that everyone in the store is staring at you, drawing conclusions about your effectiveness as a parent. "What kind of mother could that be?" you imagine people saying. "She can't control her own kid. People like that shouldn't be allowed to shop in stores." Worse yet, some may actually say these things aloud or offer you advice.

Restaurants: Here there are no aisles to scurry down and hide in. You're right out in the open, in the middle of a roomful of people who are trying to enjoy a meal they are paying for. You're very aware that your child may be ruining it for everyone. Parents of highly active, poorly adaptable, low-threshold, or irregular children find eating out very trying. Imagine a meal in a restaurant when some or all of the following things occur:

• Your child won't enter the restaurant at all, even though you selected one with little child-sized cars to sit in and drive while you eat. When you try to get your child through the doorway he screams, "No, no, no!" and, red-faced, you back away from the sight of fifty other children happily eating lunch.

• Your child, after looking forward to the outing, now refuses to eat, saying he's not hungry.

• Your child can't make up her mind what she wants.

• Your child protests at the sight of square pizza, because he's accustomed to triangular slices.

• Your child refuses to sit in his chair and wanders around a fast-food restaurant, annoying the other children by trying to take away their food.

• Your child throws his food or spills his drink.

• Your child, if the situation really escalates, kicks the waitress or goes into a full tantrum.

• Your child misbehaves so much that you start to yell at him in the restaurant, and you are aware of everyone glaring at you.

Similar reactions may occur when anything new and public is tried for the first time, or even during subsequent visits. Some children *never* get used to new situations and are always initially upset or overstimulated (or both). The circus, a movie, a live children's show, even an innocent little local puppet show may provoke reactions. Unfortunately, these reactions cannot always be accurately predicted. *All* situations may not cause these responses, but if not all, then which ones? Many of the things most children find wonderfully exciting may greatly upset a difficult child, but since you want your child to participate in the world of children, you keep trying to find the things he will enjoy. It can be a discouraging quest.

Neighbors: The often strange and incomprehensible behavior of their difficult child is something many parents want to hide. But neighbors will observe the strange dressing habits of a low-threshold child who may wear the same clothes for days on end or wear summer clothes in the dead of winter. Neighbors hear the screams of very intense children and may observe temper tantrums. They also see parents who seem to cater to the children's peculiarities, and this makes the entire family seem "weird." Parents are at a loss because they cannot explain their child's behavior reasonably to people who observe it daily. The attitude of neighbors is a sore point with many parents of difficult children.

Peers: What happens with the difficult child and his playmates? Some are fine; others have trouble. Active, disorganized, excitable children may have problems. They have trouble controlling their impulses and grab other children's toys; and if they are not adaptable, they don't share easily. This can lead to wild behavior and hitting or even biting. (Biting is one of the most mortifying experiences for a mother because it appears to be such a primitive, aggressive act. Mothers of these children are invariably embarrassed and other mothers may even ostracize the child.) The child with initial withdrawal may remain on the fringes of the group for a long time. Later, if he finds something that really interests him, he may get locked into an activity and ignore the other children. A child with a low sensory threshold, who always wears the same shirt or refuses to dress in warm winter clothes, may be teased by her peers.

One-to-one play relationships may be better because the active child will be less stimulated and the shy child not as threatened. However, sharing and taking turns still may cause problems.

Parents are so eager for their child to be "accepted" and "liked," to find friends, that this is often the hardest by-product of a difficult temperament for them. They wonder if their child is perceived as being "different" and "weird," even by other children.

Playgrounds: If the active child is taken to a playground, the results may be better since it's generally okay if children run wild there and release some of their energy. But if they begin to struggle with another child over a toy or activity, loss of control may result in hitting, kicking, or throwing sand. A very active, overstimulated child may grab toys from other children and refuse to give them up.

A child who generally withdraws and has a low threshold may cry or tantrum on being taken to a playground. Eventually she gets used to it, but then absolutely refuses to come home. Mothers whose children react in such ways find that it can be as embarrassing as the child who runs wild.

PLAY GROUPS AND NURSERY SCHOOLS

Mothers of many difficult children find that the children are better behaved when they, the mothers, are not around. The established habit patterns of the vicious circle are absent with the teacher. If you've noticed that your child is *better behaved* in school, this is the reason why. As you know, the trouble starts when he gets home.

The adjustment of difficult children to nursery school depends on how their school situation affects their temperament. And this depends on the constellation of characteristics that make up the child. Some children have no problems; others have different types of problems:

- *The highly active and distractible child.* Problems include excitability, impulsiveness, getting revved up and hitting, problems with listening and paying attention to the teacher, standing on line, and following directions. Oddly enough, these children perform well in school interviews because they are usually outgoing, and they do well in one-to-one situations.

• *The low-threshold child.* Sensitivity to bright lights, loud sounds, and overstimulation resulting from a large class of children can lead to problems in behavior.

• *The shy, poorly adaptable child.* There are problems with leaving the mother each day, problems making transitions and establishing routines, and trouble with sharing. These children do *not* do well in school interviews, because they cling and act fearful.

• *The persistent child* will be stubborn and argumentative. Teachers will say that he always wants his own way.

• *The intense child* will put extra pressure on the teachers because the loudness is so disruptive.

The result of these school behaviors may be that teachers begin to hint to parents about psychological problems, or "hyperactivity," which of course leads to parental anxiety. Parents get called into conferences with teachers and then get angry at their child for such "bad behavior," and this only makes the child's behavior worse.

PEDIATRICIANS

The first doctor you've seen with your difficult infant is the pediatrician. After the diagnosis of colic has been dismissed (because colic usually ceases at around 3 or 4 months), your doctor may have told you, "This is a perfectly normal child. You'll just have to learn to live with her."

Some doctors don't fully understand the concept of temperament, and being inexperienced in this area, they may not know anything more to tell you. They see that the child is normal, and they don't see any reasons for her behavior. In fact, except for the very active child, the doctor doesn't even *see* the behavior. But you are responsible for the patient-doctor relationship as well. Mothers often are afraid of being judged by the pediatrician. They don't want to look bad and therefore are not as direct and forthcoming about the child's behavior as they should be. And if the doctor himself can't see the behavior and you don't describe it in detail, he will be more likely to assume that *you* are the problem.

If your doctor accepts your description and talks to you about your child's *innately difficult behavior,* then he knows something about temperament and will be able to offer some constructive advice. If he doesn't understand this, he may assume that the child is simply reacting to a poor home situation.

Another problem for the busy pediatrician, even one who understands temperament, is lack of time. Unless the mother makes a separate appointment for herself, she and the doctor may never get around to discussing fully the child's behavior and what to do about it.

In this chapter and the previous one we have examined the impact the difficult child has on his environment, from his mother and father to his siblings, extended family, playmates, teachers, neighbors, and doctors. Parents of a very difficult child cannot cope with the child at home, and often they cannot cope with the child in the outside world. Their child's behavior seems to affect just about everything in their lives. In their search for answers, they have been told to "live with it." In their search for answers, they have been told, "You're too anxious, you're upsetting this child." In their search for answers, they have been told, "You really shouldn't handle him that way, you're really messing it up, doing it wrong, screwing up your kid." So they become afraid, ashamed, guilty, and angry.

No parents want to believe there is something seriously wrong with either them or their child. And in the case of the difficult child, it simply isn't true.

4

BUT IS HE "HYPERACTIVE"?

When I ask parents what the term "hyperactive" means to them, they respond with a welter of negative words. "Destructive" is a common reply, followed by "disturbed," "antisocial," "anxious," "inattentive," "learning disabled," or simply "bad."

This confusion reflects the lack of agreement about the diagnosis of "hyperactivity" in the professional community. A variety of terms, used interchangeably or overlapping with "hyperactivity," can be found in the professional literature. These include *organicity, minimal brain dysfunction, hyperkinetic syndrome, learning disability, minimal brain damage, the clumsy child, dyslexia,* and *attention deficit disorder* (*with* or *without hyperactivity*). Just as professionals were becoming used to this latest term it was discarded. We now have *attention deficit hyperactivity disorder* and *undifferentiated attention deficit disorder*!

What does this mean? And what should you do if someone tells you that your child is "hyperactive"?

THE PROBLEMS OF DIAGNOSIS

The diagnosis of "hyperactivity" is particularly problematic in preschool children. Various groups of professionals, such as pediatricians, educators, psychiatrists, neurologists, educational psychologists, and therapists of various persuasions, have used different criteria to define the syndrome and to differentiate it from normality at one end and from more serious disorders at the other. The diagnostic criteria for *attention deficit hyper-*

activity disorder are relatively clearly spelled out. However, these are largely dependent on descriptions of the child's behavior provided by parents and teachers. As such they are quite subjective. There is no such thing as a "test for hyperactivity."

"Hyperactivity" is also viewed differently in other countries. Some older studies in the United States identified between 10 and 20 percent of all school-age children as "hyperactive." Current estimates, based on stricter criteria, range from 3 to 5 percent of young children. In Great Britain and continental Europe, an even more conservative approach to diagnosis results in far fewer children being labeled.

The trend among experienced professionals, especially in the medical community, is clearly toward greater conservatism and stricter criteria in arriving at a diagnosis. This is surely positive, but professionals as a group have a way to go before they can agree on what "hyperactivity" is, especially in the young child.

As you already know my own view of normality is a broad one. I believe that a wide range of behavioral styles falls within the range of normality. I am therefore exceedingly cautious in my approach to diagnosing a *disorder* in a young child.

The word "hyperactive" can be used in two ways. One can look at it simply as an adjective that describes one dimension of behavior. If used this way, without any emotional overtones, the term carries no special meaning except that of a very high activity level. The common use of the term, however, is as a *diagnosis*. This implies abnormality and immediately leads us into a thicket of conflicting opinions.

THE PLIGHT OF THE PARENTS

Part of the problem stems from the parents' troubled search for an answer to the question "What is wrong with my child?" If the mother and father are having a problem controlling their child and their lives are being made miserable, it is in many ways more comforting to know that the child is *not* normal, because it takes the onus off them. After all, if the doctor says, "He's normal, you'll have to cope," then what do you do? This can lead to a helpless attitude, a self-pitying, martyrish frame of mind, and a withdrawal from seeking any kind of help. And from the child's point of view, how do you grow up with the identity of a cross that has to be borne?

In an effort to find out if there is anything the matter with a child who cannot seem to keep still and whose behavior seems disorganized, the parents can get on a diagnostic merry-go-round. They may go from doctor to doctor and from specialist to specialist and end up more confused. In a few of these instances, the child may be diagnosed on the basis of very little information.

Particularly in the early years of the child's development, parents may get different opinions from professionals who view the child in different settings. A pediatrician seeing the child in a busy office diagnoses "attention deficit disorder"; a nursery school teacher who observes the child in an unruly classroom calls him "hyperactive" and vaguely mentions that he will "have to be watched for learning disability"; a psychologist or psychiatrist to whom the child is referred decides he's very active but not "hyper" and talks of emotional and family problems; while a neurologist, meeting with the child on a one-to-one basis after a quiet wait in his serene outer office, says he is "normal." Who is right? If even competent professionals cannot agree on criteria, this calls into question the validity of the diagnosis itself, especially when we are dealing with a young child.

One can certainly sympathize with the plight of parents in search for answers. Our impulse as parents is to identify what's wrong and get the best help possible. In many ways, therefore, parents can be more comfortable with a diagnosis, even with the implication of abnormality. After all, the alternative can seem worse: if there is nothing wrong with the child, then either they have to learn to live with the situation or accept the blame for his behavior. "If there's nothing wrong with him it must be our fault" is a common reaction.

Thus the parents of a so-called hyperactive young child can be caught in a double bind. The implications of normality can be just as difficult to bear as those of abnormality.

THE HYPERACTIVE DILEMMA

As you can see, the term "hyperactive" has become a catch-all for many sorts of behavioral and educational dysfunctions, as well as a buzz word to single out one aspect of a child's more complicated behavior. Hyperactivity, in and of itself, should not be a diagnosis but rather a description of a specific behavior, pointing out that a child seems to move around much more than the average.

In fact, hyperactivity and normality should not be viewed as static concepts but dynamic ones. This means that a young child in particular may not be hyperactive in all situations or in the same situation at different times, and that his activity level may fall on a spectrum from moderate to high to "hyper" depending on the environment, the time of day, the child's mood, and the way he is handled. In other words, at times he may look "normal"; at other times, "hyper."

Let's look at a few examples of what I mean by a *dynamic* concept.

"But the Doctor Says He's Hyper!"

Jeremy is a 5-year-old boy, loud, excitable, often very restless, whose doctor has called him "hyperactive." Each time Jeremy's mother brings him to the doctor's office, Jeremy gets charged up in the waiting room. He has trouble sitting still when there is nothing to do, and Jeremy's doctor has a busy, crowded office with long waiting times. While there, Jeremy engages in rough play with some of the other children. By the time the doctor is ready to see Jeremy, the child is overstimulated, hyped up, and wriggling like a fish. There is no doubt in the doctor's mind that this is a hyperactive child. Jeremy's mother, however, tells the doctor she can't understand why the boy is so "good" at home when he is playing in his room. She thinks a hyperactive child is

supposed to be hyper *all* the time, but Jeremy spends
long, quiet times playing with his sets of Lego blocks.
Also, while last year in nursery school he was often
wild, this year he is in a small kindergarten class with a
calm, patient teacher and is doing much better. When
Jeremy's mother explains this to the pediatrician, he
seems skeptical. Is Jeremy hyperactive? Is he sometimes
hyperactive? Is he normal or not? Is he sometimes abnormal? Is that possible?

The Tomboy

Claire is a 6-year-old who does not seem to have too
many behavioral problems—except in school. She is having trouble in her parochial school first-grade class because, the teachers tell her mother, she does not follow
directions, she refuses to stand on line and pushes to the
front, and she gets very excited during play periods and
has hit or kicked other children. The teachers suggest to
Claire's mother that the child be taken to a psychologist
or psychiatrist and evaluated since these are signs that
she could have an emotional problem. Claire's mother is
puzzled; Claire is her fourth child, the other three are
boys, and her daughter has never seemed "hyperactive"
or troubled to her. If Claire hits one of her brothers, he
hits her back; she has never appeared to be any more
active than the boys. She knows that Claire is not an
obedient, quiet child, but this has never seriously troubled her. So what if the child runs from one activity to
another and doesn't sit and play with dolls? Claire's
mother does not want to see a professional, but the
school keeps pressing and indicates that further, more
serious issues may emerge if Claire is not "given help."
Is Claire hyperactive, or is her behavior simply more
noticeable in school? Here is a clear example of how the
same behavior can be viewed as normal or abnormal,
depending on the setting.

"He's Usually So Good"

On the day before school opens, the big local shoe store
is generally a madhouse. Mothers must wait as long as

two hours before their children are fitted for new school shoes. Most parents try to avoid this scene, but if the family has been on vacation, it is sometimes unavoidable. Stevie, aged 3½, is generally a moderately active, happy child, occasionally prone to outbursts. Stevie's mother is taking him to the store to buy a pair of sneakers for nursery school. When they arrive, they take a number: 132. The salespeople are waiting on 45 and 46. Stevie's mother decides to leave and return later; she takes Stevie into a nearby shop to buy some new polo shirts for him. He is getting fidgety by now; his mother promises an ice cream cone after the shoes are purchased. They return to the store and take seats. As the time passes, Stevie gets increasingly upset and squirmy; he leaves his chair repeatedly and cruises around the store. Soon he is bumping into other customers and colliding with the busy shoe salesmen. He gets more and more revved up, and finally there's an outburst. He has grabbed a toy away from another child, and when the child tries to take it back, he pushes her to the ground. His mother, embarrassed and aware of the stares of everyone in the store, tries to take the toy away. A full-blown tantrum follows. Finally she grabs him and drags him from the shoe store. She can hear two mothers sitting near the door talking about her. "Poor woman," they are saying. "Her kid is hyperactive."

Let's look at this last case of a moderately active, clearly normal child, Stevie. His behavior does not ordinarily fit any definition of hyperactivity, yet when he has been asked to wait for a long time after the boring routine of shopping, when he is confined to a chair in a crowded shoe store, when he gets overstimulated and cranky, his behavior becomes wild. But does one call this child "hyperactive"? Of course not! In the shoe store, however, he looks much the same as the so-called hyperactive child.

Even with a child who has been diagnosed "hyperactive," such as Jeremy, the boy who visited his pediatrician, there are always instances in which his behavior will not reflect accurately what some professionals define as hyperactivity. In some settings, such as his room at home, he is able to sit down and focus his attention on doing something he likes. With his teacher, in a calm, structured class, he is doing well, although he needs some extra attention. However, in the doctor's office, as in other overstimulating settings, his behavior deteriorates to the point where he seems "abnormal."

In Claire's case, it's interesting to note how her relaxed home environment and her position as fourth child in a family of boys have masked many of the features of the so-called hyperactive child. A poor attention span, excitability, impulsiveness, fighting, disorganized play—all would be almost lost from view in the swirl of such a household. And Claire has a mother who is experienced and calm. Try to imagine this same little girl born into a very orderly, somewhat rigid household as the first child. She would stick out like a sore thumb. Even a moderately active child might seem overactive in such a household. And the physical constraints of such a setting might exaggerate the problem. Claire and her brothers are being raised in an old, sprawling house with large, shabby, comfortable rooms and a big yard. If she were living in a small city apartment with bric-a-brac on each tabletop, her parents would be in trouble with her by the time she reached the age of 2.

In a parochial school with a rigid teacher, Claire's behavior clearly identifies her as a "problem." Yet it's virtually the same behavior that is accepted, even encouraged, at home. (This, incidentally, is a perfect illustration of a good fit at home but a very poor fit in school.) So what do we call Claire? Is she a hyperactive troublemaker, or is she a highly active tomboy who is in the wrong school for her?

The Importance of Context

These three examples clearly illustrate the two central problems with the term "hyperactivity": The younger child's activity level is almost always dependent on the broader context; and the dividing line between normal and abnormal behavior, at best hard to define, is often in the eye of the beholder. We are dealing with activity level on an easy-to-difficult spectrum ranging from low to very high. Virtually no child is wildly active all the time. The child interacts with his environment. In different settings and under different sets of circumstances, an extremely active child can be calm, or a moderately active child can get wildly overstimulated. The time of day can come into play—many children pass through a period of time each day their mothers call the "witching hour," when their behavior is well-nigh impossible. Hunger or diet can affect behavior, as many parents intuitively know. How much sleep the child has had is also important. Ask the mothers of toddlers what their children are like when they skip a nap at the age of 2. And any child who feels anxious or threatened can manifest extreme behavior. Can anyone say for a fact that a screaming, actively tantruming child in the doorway of a supermarket is a hyperactive child being restrained by his parents, or a child who dislikes anything new and overwhelming being forced to enter a hectic, strange place? To a passerby, the final behavior looks identical, and the parents appear to be incapable of "controlling" the child.

Let's examine what can happen in some school settings. Because of the shortage of educational funds, many schools have fewer teachers and larger classes. There may be more unruly behavior in such a setting, and in fact, a few years ago, in some schools "hyperactivity" was virtually synonymous with unruly behavior. The child displaying such behavior, for whatever reason, especially a child who was unable to keep up with the class, was all too often called "hyperactive." And these children were too often put on medication. There has been a backing off from this position of late, but not enough, and in some places these practices still exist.

Thus there are many reasons to question the use of the term "hyperactivity":

1. One characteristic, really an adjective, should not be used to describe the total child.

2. The boundaries of normality are hard to define. "Different" is not the same as "abnormal."

3. The setting of the behavior is very important. This is especially pertinent when the behavior is most evident in school.

4. The age of the child is important. Since a 2-year-old is ordinarily more active than a 4-year-old, the boundaries between moderate, high and very high activity levels tend to blur at a younger age. In an older child this distinction is easier to make. Professionals should exercise much more caution in diagnosing "hyperactivity" in very young children; and good professionals are doing just that.

5. Time of day plays a role. A child during the "witching hour," a hungry child, or one who has not napped may get "hyper" as a result. And just as adults experience cyclical biorhythms in their daily behavior, so do children. Is your child a "day" person or a "night" person? These ups and downs can affect his activity level.

6. Diet plays a role as well. Many mothers have observed their child's reaction to sugary foods or to foods with additives, and an increasing number of physicians are recognizing the link between nutrition and behavior.

7. Most importantly, who is making the diagnosis and what are the criteria? The psychiatrist may have one set of criteria, the pediatrician another, the neurologist still another. Objective criteria for defining "abnormal" behavior are much harder to arrive at in toddlers than in older children. Doctors should only make a diagnosis based on a full objective evaluation, and any diagnosis is only as valid as the criteria used to make it.

A NEW PERSPECTIVE: BRINGING IN TEMPERAMENT

If we stop looking at the young child as "hyperactive" and instead think of him as a *difficult child with a very high activity level,* new horizons open. We can begin to look at the total child, not just at one characteristic, and offer him and the family help without the pitfalls of diagnostic labels.

Keep in mind that activity level is just one of the nine dimensions of temperament. So-called hyperactive children are *not* just highly active. They are also temperamentally difficult in other ways. They are distractible. They are usually poorly adaptable and have trouble with changes and transitions. They are frequently persistent and stubborn. They are highly intense—loud and excitable. Their rhythms of sleep and appetite are often irregular. Their threshold may be low—to loud noise, bright lights, the feel of clothes—and generally they are easily overstimulated. (Usually, however, these children are forward-going rather than shy, and their disposition is sunny and cheerful.)

With so many difficult characteristics, it makes a good deal of sense to include many if not most so-called hyperactive children under the general rubric of temperamentally difficult children.

Think of what would happen if another difficult trait were used to define the whole child:

Louise withdraws from new situations. At the age of 3½, she has so much trouble with new places, new people, and new things that her mother has problems taking her anywhere. She cowers, clings to her mother fiercely, or screams. When Louise was taken to see a psychologist whose office she had never visited, and met the doctor, a total stranger, she withdrew at once. Based on one visit, the psychologist erroneously could call this child "anxious"—but a good psychologist probably would not, since this determination shouldn't be made on the basis of a single visit. Certainly no one would speak of a "hyperwithdrawn child" the way one speaks of a hyperactive child. Nor would we call the child who is subject to the temperamental feature of negative mood "depressed" or "hypernegative" because he is serious, rarely smiles, and may be crabby and sulky. (It is important to emphasize here that *negative mood is not depression.* Clinical depression in children shows itself in persistent sadness, loss of appetite, sleep disturbances, low energy levels, and in other symptoms that we find also in adult depression.)

If no other characteristic defines a child's condition, why should activity level?

The Story of Joshua: A Broader View

Let's look at an ordinary incident involving a little boy who has been diagnosed as "hyperactive" by his pediatrician. And as we watch him, let's also see how his other temperamental features come into play. Remember that very active children stand out because of their wild behavior, but if you look carefully, you'll see that there's a great deal more going on.

Joshua has been invited to a birthday party for a playmate of his from the 4-year-old group at nursery school. His mother, who is extremely affectionate and caring with her young son, is concerned about his frequently wild and disruptive behavior and does not often take him to such parties. But this is a party for Joshua's closest school friend, so she has accepted. Her concern for Joshua's condition has not been alleviated by a visit to a neurologist, who has found nothing wrong. The pediatrician's opinion seems to be borne out by much of Joshua's behavior.

However, in quiet surroundings at home, Joshua can sit and listen quietly to a record. In fact, when it's a record he particularly likes, he pays very close attention (he is *persistent*). But on the day of the party, his mother makes the mistake of interrupting his record-listening abruptly to tell him it's time to get dressed. He is now *locked in* to this activity and does not want to be disturbed. The conflict escalates, and Joshua starts to scream loudly (he is a *high-intensity* child). When he calms down, his mother brings out the new outfit she has bought for the party, but Joshua insists he wants to wear his old clothing because he is used to it (*poor adaptability*) and because it feels better: he says the new clothes are too tight and itch (he has a *low sensory threshold* to touch). When his mother forces him to wear the clothes after a long struggle, he has a tantrum. Finally she relents and allows him to wear his worn-out sneakers instead of his dress-up shoes. By the time they are ready to leave the house, both mother and child are upset and on edge. They have had several power struggles already and they're not even out the door!

When they get to the party, they find several children already there, playing happily. As children and mothers keep arriving, the party gets louder and busier, the volume rising and the activity mounting. The children chase around, batting at the silver helium balloons that dangle ribbons from the ceiling; the party child's father is taking flash pictures. Distracted and overstimulated by the noise, the lights, the excited children, and the milling adults, Joshua begins to get very "revved up"; his mother sees the danger signs but hopes that soon the children will be called to sit down quietly at lunch. (Joshua's reaction to the party brings in his *distractibility* and *low sensory threshold* to noise, lights, and general overstimulation.)

When the children are all seated for lunch and are examining their party hats, horns, and bags of favors, Joshua refuses to take his chair and continues to roam about the house and touch all the toys, books, games, and birthday gifts within his reach. He tells his mother he doesn't want to eat because he isn't hungry (and he isn't; he has *irregular rhythms*). His presence is starting to disturb the other children at the party. His mother coaxes him into a corner and sits him down with a toy record player not unlike the one he has at home. He continues to wiggle around and tries to get up and run again, but his mother soothes him and finds one of his favorite records among his friend's. As Joshua is beginning to settle a little, the magic show is announced and his mother abruptly shuts off the machine and takes it away. Joshua gets wild (his *poor adaptability* makes it almost impossible for him to shift gears so quickly). He begins to run around the group of seated children, disrupting the show, yanking at the other children's hair, clothes, party favors. Another child pulls his party horn away, and Joshua loses control and kicks the child. His mother, who has had enough and who is horribly ashamed, picks up this squirming, screaming child and hauls him away, thinking that her pediatrician was dead right and the neurologist didn't know what he was talking about. The other parents at the party couldn't agree with the pediatrician more; this, they all agree, is a hyperactive kid.

But we can see, by breaking down all of Joshua's smaller actions and looking at them one at a time, that it was a constellation of difficult traits that created Joshua's behavior, not only the one characteristic of high activity. Activity level most often gets singled out because it's the *most socially visible* trait. It's what makes the child stand out in the crowd, and it's also the easiest to pinpoint. How many observers know or understand the concepts of low sensory threshold or irregular rhythms? And even the most sensitive of parents often is not aware of the problems caused by a child's poor adaptability.

It should be obvious by now that there are many aspects to these children's behavior; learning to manage them is dependent on understanding their *total* temperament. View them as difficult children and you can learn to cope with them.

WHEN IS A DIAGNOSIS NEEDED?

A diagnostic label can be appropriate for some children: a child who is extremely active no matter where he is; who virtually never sits still; whose actions are haphazard rather than goal-directed; who is always touching things; who has trouble paying attention to almost anything; who does not follow instructions; who is always interrupting; who is impulsive and loses control very easily. Such a child deserves a proper evaluation by a competent medical professional and may well be appropriately diagnosed as having "attention deficit hyperactivity disorder."

If we don't have yet another confusing change in terminology, the chances are good that various professionals will come to agree more on the behavioral descriptions needed to arrive at this diagnosis. At least then we will all mean much the same thing when we refer to "attention deficit hyperactivity disorder" (ADHD) in an elementary school-age child. This is a clear advantage, even in the absence of an objective test, as long as we remember that the diagnosis of ADHD represents a convenient way of grouping a set of difficult behaviors.

Although interesting research is being conducted into the biochemical and neurophysiological basis of behavior, there is no clear evidence that ADHD is a true medical condition. Children who warrant this diagnosis are much more likely to be boys. They also show an increase, compared to other children, in associated features such as:

- a history of pregnancy and birth complications
- delayed language development
- specific learning disabilities emerging at school age
- problems with coordination
- a family history of similar problems
- motor tics (involuntary twitching)

Such a child certainly needs to be evaluated properly and may then need language therapy, occupational therapy for the motor problems, a good tutor, a resource room, or even a special class.

A trial of medication may also be warranted. Remember always that medication should never be the only treatment, and that it can be discontinued, also on a trial basis, once things are going well. In general, these medications (e.g., Ritalin, Cylert) have proved to be effective and quite safe in school-age children. In the case of a preschool child, medication should be considered only as a last resort if behavioral methods of management have failed. (For a more complete exploration of the medication issue, refer to Chapter 11.) You will require the services of one or more specialists. Make certain that these professionals coordinate their activities. One of them should serve as overseer; a good pediatrician is the natural person for this function.

One more note of caution, however: The field of *learning disabilities* has become an industry with social, political and economic ramifications. The term itself is, if anything, more overused than "hyperactivity," and generates just as much parental confusion and anxiety. A parent whose child is having a problem with learning, even a minor one, can easily enter a network of specialists who come armed with a bewildering array of sophisticated tests often leading to impressions and prescriptions that sound both vague and ominous. The very word "disability" implies that something is seriously wrong.

Once again, we need a much more conservative attitude. Most certainly, there is a group of truly learning-disabled children. They require the specialized services of competent professionals who follow strict criteria in arriving at their diagnosis. However, there are many more children experiencing some learning problems who perhaps just process information differently. They may need some help but in no way should be categorized as "learning disabled."

As I pointed out at the beginning of this chapter, "hyperactive" is an adjective. It describes behavior; it does not define the cause of that behavior. Hyperactive behavior can be due to something other than temperament: brain damage, severe emotional or mental disorder, or physical illness; and in those instances, a full diagnostic evaluation and specialized help *must* be sought.

For the majority of children who warrant the diagnosis of "attention deficit hyperactivity disorder," even those who need other forms of help, the knowledge to be gained from understanding the other temperamental factors can help you, as a parent, to cope better and to manage your child's behavior more successfully. (Guidelines to seeking further professional help for these children will be found in Chapter 11.)

5

A DAY IN THE LIFE OF A DIFFICULT CHILD

The story you are about to read is that of a *very* difficult child, a real mother-killer. Few children are as hard to raise as this one. But the difference is in the degree of difficulty, not in its basic elements, and I use this extreme example to highlight traits you may recognize in your less difficult child.

✦

When Adam Johnson was born, his mother, Marjorie, anticipated an experience similar to that of raising his brother, Jeremy. She was a bit disappointed when she learned she had another boy, because she felt girls were "easier." But she was delighted that the baby was healthy and she settled in for a comfortable hospital stay, feeling much the experienced mother who could handle another boy with ease.

She had some trouble feeding Adam during the hospital stay; later, at home, he didn't get onto a schedule as easily as Jeremy had. He always seemed fretful when he was with her, and he would fall into short catnaps from which he would awaken easily, with a start, accompanied by loud cries. He seemed louder than Jeremy, but his mother felt this was because she was used to a quieter, older child (Jeremy was 3). Adam's father, Stephen, was proud of his new son and called this behavior "feisty" and "tough," predicting that Adam would be a "little pisser."

Neither parent could have anticipated what was to happen to Adam and to their family. Adam Johnson's

problems with eating, sleeping, and crying were only the
beginning. His fretful, cranky, erratic behavior continued to increase, and, by 2 months, his parents went
nights without any restful sleep. Adam woke up continually and never seemed to stop crying. He cried loudly
after he was fed and *after* he was changed. He was
generally squirmy and irritable, and holding him didn't
seem to help. Rocking him didn't help, either; musical
toys didn't charm him, and rattles didn't distract him.
His mother was not surprised when the pediatrician said
he was "colicky," and she waited anxiously for the few
months to pass until it was over. But even after several
months, Adam continued his crying and poor sleep. The
doctor had no explanation; colic usually ends at 4
months. Marjorie Johnson was becoming exhausted and
edgy, and her husband was spending the worst nights
sleeping downstairs on the living room couch so he would
not be exhausted in court the next day (he had a good
practice as a lawyer).

Marjorie's mother was full of suggestions at first,
but as none worked, Marjorie felt inadequate and helpless as her mother questioned her closely and told her
she was doing things wrong. Her mother had been
overinvolved with her raising of Jeremy as well, but the
advice hadn't bothered Marjorie as much since he had
been a "good baby." Now she felt her mother was right;
she *was* doing something wrong. She was a "bad mother,"
or at least "not as good a mother as my own was." But
even though Adam's grandmother had lots of advice on
how to handle him, when she visited the family (which
was often, as she lived close by), she would not hold the
baby for a long time, nor did she offer to baby-sit. His
loudness and squirming and wiggling seemed to frighten
her. She felt she would not be able to "control him."

By the time Adam was 6 months old, his family was
clearly affected. Marjorie could not go shopping or take
Jeremy to nursery school or run her usual errands without worrying about her screaming baby and wondering
what other mothers were thinking. They always seemed
to stare at her as the baby carried on, making her feel
even more ashamed that she couldn't get him to stop.

Pacifiers did not work; Marjorie even tried a tiny amount of Scotch mixed into his orange juice. Nothing helped to calm him down, it seemed. And the marriage was suffering. Marjorie was constantly tired, Stephen was impatient with her, and they often quarreled over how to handle the problems. Stephen wanted Marjorie to "let the baby cry it out" and "leave him alone," but Marjorie believed that there was something wrong with the baby and "he needed help," so how could you simply let him scream?

As Adam grew older, the parents began noticing a change in their older child. Jeremy was a friendly, contented child who enjoyed playing outside in their yard or in his room, humming to himself as he worked with his Lego blocks or played in the sandbox. The presence of the new baby was naturally disruptive for him, but as the months passed, his parents noticed more of a change. He had become worried, bothered by the baby's crying. "What's wrong with Adam?" he would ask. "Why does he cry all the time? Why is he screaming?" He would stand next to the crib and try to get the baby to stop fretting. Marjorie noticed that Jeremy clung to her more when they went out and that he no longer liked to play alone but continually asked his parents to come and "help" him. Adam's needs left her little time for Jeremy, and she wondered if all this stress was going to harm him as well. This feeling only added to the burden of caring for this "impossible" baby.

When Adam began to walk, at about the age of 1 year, there was already a good deal of strain on the marriage and tension in the household. And Adam's walking, or rather running (which is what he seemed to do as soon as he got to his feet), complicated matters even more, for he was a holy terror. The house had to be babyproofed beyond anything required for Jeremy three years earlier. And the disruptions of sleeping and eating continued, complicated by problems dressing Adam, chasing Adam, and controlling Adam. He was impervious to discipline. Marjorie stopped thinking of him as "helpless" and "troubled" and started thinking of him as a "little monster" who "did things on purpose."

By the time Adam was 3 life in the Johnson home revolved around him. He was often wild and never seemed to listen. Repeated power struggles would usually end in tantrums. He slept a great deal or very little without any predictable pattern. He could not be easily fed, for it was hard to get him to sit still at the table and even harder to find foods he liked. He refused to wear any clothes he called "itchy," which included anything new, and he liked to sleep in what he was wearing. He never wore pajamas. He never sat still to play with games or puzzles, but only to watch MTV with its flashy, loud rock videos running continuously. His father hated this and tried to get Adam interested in watching sports. But Adam had no patience for baseball and would scream for MTV until his father, in disgust, changed the channel.

The constant battles were taking their toll on Adam as well as his family. Adam was becoming fearful at night and clinging more to his mother. In nursery school he was somewhat calmer but certainly still a handful. On the positive side, Adam, when not angry or upset, seemed to have a cheerful disposition. And his father enjoyed roughhousing with him and was proud of Adam's "toughness." His mother liked his "creativity." He loved drawing colorful pictures of flowers and cars.

On an ordinary day in the life of the Johnson family, Adam was always at center stage, and his parents, brother, grandparents, friends, schoolmates, and teachers were all supporting players. It sometimes seemed to his mother that the world revolved around her difficult child and his bad behavior, and in a sense it did—for everyone reacted to his actions, which were often negative and which left a string of negative reactions in their wake.

Stephen Johnson's clock radio clicked on at 6:00 A.M. on weekdays. He would rise and head into the shower, while Marjorie took a moment to collect herself and prepare for the struggle she knew awaited her. It was always hardest to start in the morning, because that's when she had to realize, all over again, that nothing would have changed or passed in the night. Adam would be the same that morning as he had been yesterday

morning, and all of this wasn't simply going to go away,
like a bad dream.

She rose from bed and went down the hall to the
second bathroom to brush her teeth. Then she tapped on
Jeremy's door but did not check to see if he was up. The
fuss that Adam made in the morning would wake him
up anyway. She took a deep breath and went into Adam's room. The chaos of his jumbled possessions always
leaped out at her. She liked things to be orderly, and in
fact Jeremy was just like her in this respect, keeping his
books and games sorted out neatly. Adam didn't keep
his hands off anything he could reach, and it was only
after she bought Jeremy a wall unit with locked doors
on the bottom and high shelves on top that he could
keep his things from his brother. She stepped around the
piles of blocks and toy trucks and cars and moved to the
bed. She had given up putting sheets and blankets over
Adam because he was always hot and moved around in
his sleep; now he had only a quilt, which was pushed in
a heap off the bottom of the bed. He lay sprawled on his
side, his legs bent as if he were leaping over a fence. His
mother hesitated before waking him. It was only quiet
in the house when he was asleep. But they needed extra
time in the morning; otherwise he would be late for
nursery school.

As hard as it was to get him to go to bed, it was
harder to get him going in the morning. She roused him
and he sat up and rubbed his eyes. She gave him a kiss
and it began. "Go into the bathroom and brush your
teeth," she told him. He leaped off the bed and began to
play with the toys on the floor. She repeated her request.
He didn't respond. She opened his dresser drawers and
took out clean clothing. He was wearing sweat pants
and a sweat shirt he'd had on the day before. Marjorie
fixed a smile on her face. "Let's put on this nice clean
T-shirt and blue jeans," she said. "No," said Adam. She
bargained some more. Adam refused. The sweat suit was
stained and rumpled. She made a grab for the sleeves, to
pull the top over his head. He yowled and tore his arms
from her grip. Sighing, she put the clean clothing down
and started to work on getting him to brush his teeth.

She did not understand why getting him to do things was such a chore; all she knew was that from the time he got up in the morning it was one battle after another.

After tying and retying his sneaker laces several times to get them "right," Marjorie turned her attention, briefly, to Jeremy, who had washed and dressed himself and was playing in his room. Sometimes she felt her older son was too quiet and too good; she wished he would be more mischievous. But the times he disobeyed were so infrequent and so much a reaction to Adam getting all the attention that she knew they were going to have problems with Jeremy when he got older. It was impossible to spare enough time or attention for him now, and this only added to her feelings of guilt and inadequacy as a mother.

Down in the kitchen, Stephen had put on a pot of coffee for breakfast, and she gratefully took a cup while she set out cereal, butter, sugar, and milk on the table. Mealtimes were often wrecked by Adam's behavior, but there were days when breakfast was easier than lunch or dinner. Adam was often hungry in the morning, and he seemed to like his breakfast foods more than other meals. He always ate a sugared cereal with lots of milk and several handfuls of raisins. He chopped at the cereal with his spoon until it was mushy, then ate the raisins one by one before eating the soggy cereal. He liked the same bowl each morning, an old one from his babyhood with a teddy bear on the bottom.

Adam came down late for breakfast, after repeated calls and warnings about being late for nursery school. Stephen finished his breakfast and left to drive to the railroad station. Jeremy went to his school bus stop, and Marjorie left Adam in the kitchen for a moment while she went upstairs to change into a pair of pants and a shirt to drive him to nursery school. When she returned downstairs, she saw that he had opened the refrigerator and had emptied a quart of milk into his cereal bowl and all over the kitchen table. He was happily splashing in the milk on the floor. Impatient, she pulled him away, yelling, "You're a bad child, a very bad boy!" She always found herself screaming at Adam louder than she had with Jeremy; she felt so tense and wound up when she dealt with Adam and, worse, she didn't think he listened to her. She thought if she didn't yell and scream he wouldn't hear her at all. As usual when she yelled, Adam screamed right back at her, "You're a dope, *you* clean it up!"

During the ride to the nursery school, which Adam attended three mornings a week, she calmed down and was able to enjoy her child's company. Adam liked riding in the car and for a few minutes his mother could pretend he was just like the other kids, companionable, pleasant, and easy to be with. She smiled at him and reached over to give his hand a squeeze. When he was like this, she could relax and feel good about him. And when he smiled back at her, he was charming. That was the funny part about Adam. With all the problems he had doing ordinary things, he was still a likable child, at least some of the time.

When they arrived at school, Marjorie knew she would have to be firm with him because he didn't like to switch what he was doing, and getting out of the car usually caused a big fuss. His mother opened the car door and reached in to grab his arm to pull him out. She did this quickly, because her son's tantrums in front of the school embarrassed her a great deal. Other children skipped up the front walk and into the building; Adam dragged his feet, yelled, and cried. Once he got inside and saw the children running around, he got excited and threw himself enthusiastically into their play. But getting him there was often a huge job.

Adam spent the next three hours with a group of fifteen 3- to 4-year-old children. He enjoyed active play, but his teachers always kept an eye on him because if he got too excited, he would strike out. He had hit and kicked several children already, and in spite of having been told that this kind of behavior was not tolerated, he could not seem to help himself. When he got over-stimulated, he would interrupt other children, try to grab their toys, or even lash out. The teachers had learned to give him extra time to quiet down before they tried to move him from one routine to another. But what his teachers could not handle was his "refusal" to follow rules; each school day they tried to get him to sit still or stand in line with the other children. They insisted, they tried to bribe him, they punished him, they yelled at him, but nothing worked. He always wandered on the fringes of the story group or the songtime group or shot to the head of the line at the water fountain. They had spoken to his mother about this, and she had told them he could not sit for long at meals, though when he was interested in something he was playing with, he did pay attention for a longer time. Privately, his teachers agreed that when Adam attended elementary school he would have adjustment problems.

One of the activities that Adam did sit still for was drawing, and this particular day the children were given brushes and paints and asked to paint a picture of their homes. Adam worked hard on his picture and was able to draw a colorful and beautifully proportioned house. He liked making pictures at home as well, and this was something his mother enjoyed helping him with and encouraged him to do. Neither his parents nor his teachers could reconcile this creativity with his other "wild" behavior.

During playtime outside, Adam got overexcited and knocked one of the smaller boys off a swing. The child cut his knee when he fell, and Adam almost hit him in the head with the swing he'd claimed. His teacher warned him not to do that again, but he looked away and did not seem to hear. He grabbed a ball and ran away.

When school ended, Marjorie picked up Adam, who presented her with his painting of the house. She told him how pretty it was, and they shared another good moment. But then she said they had to go home a different way; she wanted to stop at the store for some milk, and Adam got upset. He liked driving the other way, he was used to it, and he began to fuss. His mother sensed trouble coming on, but she needed the milk and some other staples, so she drove to the store. Adam, locked into his frustration, continued to complain loudly, and when they got to the supermarket, his mother had to pull him from the car and force him to sit in the shopping cart. Everyone in the store seemed to stop and stare as she pushed the wagon with the howling, red-faced child in it. She could not get him to stop even when she shoved some things he liked into his hands; he threw the cookies onto the floor and shook his head at the potato chips and pretzels, building to a tantrum. Cutting the shopping trip short, she paid for a few items and carried him from the store.

The bad mood continued into lunch, which he would not touch, and through his "quiet time" in his room, during which she could hear him throwing his toys around. At one point, he began to scream and rushed from his room crying, "Mommy!" He had cut his finger slightly and panicked at the sight of the blood. His mother washed the small cut and put an elaborate bandage on it, but he still fussed over this for close to an hour. After the scene in the store, this was almost too much for Marjorie, who was expected to greet Jeremy in a little while, finish cleaning the house, prepare dinner, and then bathe both children. When Jeremy returned from school, she sent both boys into the backyard to play and collapsed into a chair, too exhausted and overwhelmed to do anything. Not a day passed that there weren't at least half a dozen crises with Adam. It was never calm. It was never quiet. And it never went smoothly.

Jeremy ran in several times to report on Adam's bad behavior: Adam took away his baseball bat, Adam ran after the neighbor's cat, Adam had kicked him. Her husband wanted to teach Jeremy to kick back, which Marjorie thought was all wrong. Stephen seemed to *like* Adam's toughness and thought Jeremy was weak and a "sissy." This confused many issues of discipline and made some of Adam's bad behavior "good," while Jeremy came out the "goody-goody." Marjorie was so confused by all this that she found herself ignoring much of the mixed-up play between the brothers, glad to have them out of her hair for a little while.

After the time outdoors, the boys came in to watch TV. There were numerous fights over what to watch because Adam always wanted only his favorite program. Marjorie often made Jeremy watch what Adam liked because Adam could stay glued to the TV for a longer time if his favorite show was on. But on this day, Jeremy insisted and they had a fight, which ended with a lamp knocked over and broken. "Wait until your father sees this!" Marjorie screamed as Stephen pulled up in his car. He walked in to find his wife yelling, his older son in tears, his youngest running around, and dinner not even begun.

Marjorie demanded that he discipline the children.

Stephen asked her why she could not. "Why aren't you able to keep these kids in line? What's the matter with you?"

She accused him of insensitivity. "I had a perfectly rotten day and you don't even care."

"Why do you have to take it out on me?" her husband said. "And why isn't the house ever straightened? Couldn't I have a drink when I come in? What's the matter with you? You can't take care of any of us!"

Marjorie stormed into the kitchen and slammed cabinet doors and rattled pots as she began dinner. Stephen told the children, "Leave me alone, get lost," and then he saw the broken lamp. He went into the dining room to the bar to get a drink.

Whenever his parents fought, Adam's behavior got worse. This evening, he took a marking pen from a drawer in the table in their hall and began to make a picture on the wallpaper. When Marjorie caught sight of this, she snatched the pen from his hand. "You horrible child, I hate you!" she screamed. "Go to your room!" Adam stood his ground and jiggled from foot to foot.

"You heard me! Get to your room!"

Adam went into the living room and turned on the TV.

"I'm going to count to three," his mother warned. "You better do what I say or I'll—" She didn't know what to threaten. Should she turn off the TV? How would she finish fixing dinner? Why wasn't her husband helping out? He had disappeared, gone upstairs to shower and change. Adam was standing in front of the television, up very close where she had warned him not to stand. He would not listen to her. It was useless.

"Adam!" she cried. "You better do what I say!" And she went back into the kitchen.

Adam remained glued to the set until dinner was ready.

When Stephen came downstairs, the broken lamp had been stored in a closet, the table was set, the boys were watching television, and he could smell something cooking in the kitchen. He thought, with some satisfaction, that this was more like it. Then he caught sight of the marking on the wallpaper and went into the kitchen to confront his wife. "When did *that,*" he asked, gesturing, "take place?"

"A little while ago," she said without looking up from the saucepan of vegetables. "I punished Adam."

"You know, he's a little boy. You really have to be tough with boys. I know all about this. I was a little boy, too. My mother says—" he began.

"I know what she says," Marjorie interrupted. "Adam is not like you. He's much worse. He doesn't listen, and he has these terrible tantrums. You should have seen what happened in the supermarket today."

"You have to be firmer with him," Stephen insisted. "He listens to me."

"You aren't around him all day," she said wearily.

"Okay, I'll take over at dinner," he said. "I'll show you how to do it."

"Good luck," Marjorie said under her breath. They were having chicken for dinner. Adam did not much like chicken, so she had made him something special, an English muffin pizza, which he enjoyed. This caused a problem with Jeremy, who also wanted his favorite food, so she had made a hot dog for Jeremy.

Stephen fixed another drink for himself, then got the boys to wash their hands. They were ready to sit down to eat. Adam refused. He wanted to watch more TV. Stephen shut it off. Adam howled a protest and turned it on. Stephen shut it off. Adam reached for the knob. His father smacked his hand, hard. Adam screamed, glared at his father, then threw himself to the ground and kicked the floor, screaming, "TV, TV, TV!"

Jeremy stared at this wide-eyed.

"Go inside and sit down for dinner," his father ordered his sons. Jeremy went, immediately. Adam kicked and screamed.

"Did you hear me?" Stephen roared. He lifted Adam up, brought him into the dining room, and planted him in a chair. Adam got up; his father forced him down. This went on for a few minutes and finally Stephen gave up. Adam rolled to the ground and continued to tantrum. Marjorie began serving dinner.

Eventually, after being ignored for five minutes, Adam quieted down and allowed himself to be placed in a chair. Swinging his legs, he kicked at the table. No one said anything. Jeremy ate his hot dog. His parents spooned out chicken and vegetables. Adam took a bite of his pizza, then spat it out.

"What's the matter?" his mother asked.

"It tastes funny!"

"It's the same you always have," Marjorie lied. She had used a different brand of tomato sauce, a new kind she had a coupon for. Adam could always tell when she changed the brand of something he liked. She couldn't fool him.

His father, exhausted from the scene before dinner, let the children leave the table to watch television. "I give up," he said.

His wife simply stared at him. He wasn't even home all day.

"You don't even know what it's like," she said, challenging him.

"Don't I? Well, you don't have to work an eight-hour day and come home to this mess," he replied.

They raised their voices. The argument they were having was one they had repeatedly, and each time it took the same pattern. They would attack each other following some misbehavior of Adam's, then Stephen would accuse Marjorie of not disciplining the child enough, and Marjorie would get overly protective and defend Adam as "the baby" and "troubled"; Stephen would follow with the accusation that Marjorie "smothered" his son, who was simply a tough, rambunctious little boy needing a firm hand to guide him as well as an occasional spanking.

"Why are you so afraid to take him down a peg?" Stephen went on. "You're his mother. You let him get away with murder! A big part of this problem is you, his mother, I can tell you that."

She threw down her fork. "Then you stay at home with him every day. You see what he does. He's not like the other kids. He's not like Jeremy was. Ask his teachers in school."

"I'm just saying that if you were tougher—"

"I'm doing the dishes and taking a bath. You be tough." Marjorie got up, shoved the door into the kitchen open, then let it swing shut behind her.

Stephen looked at his watch and decided he would begin to get the boys ready for bed.

In the living room, Adam was glued to the television. One of his favorite shows was on, a police drama with howling sirens, blazing car crashes, and screeching motorcycles.

"Adam and Jeremy," Stephen said in a loud voice over the sound of the TV, "time for bed."

Adam didn't move. Jeremy looked up and said, "Where's Mommy?"

"She's resting."

"Why? Is she mad at us?" Jeremy asked. He was a worried child, always eager to please.

"She's just tired. Now let's go upstairs."

"Mommy said we had to have a bath tonight," Jeremy said.

Stephen realized, again, what a goody-goody their older child had become. Was it because Adam was so bad and because Marjorie let him get away with so much? He got angrier with his wife.

"Come on, boys."

Adam didn't move. His father turned off the set. Adam screamed, once. It was piercing. "No, Adam. It's time to take a bath, and then we're going to bed."

"No!" Adam screamed.

His father picked him up. Adam began to thrash and kick, then bit his father on the hand. "You little—" his father began, then slapped Adam on the face. Adam hurled himself to the floor, screaming and kicking. Jeremy stood to one side, watching. "Mommy won't like this," he said. "She lets him watch whatever he wants."

"Well, I don't," Stephen said. He picked Adam up, stayed clear of the flailing arms and legs, and carried him up the stairs. He put him on the floor of the bathroom. The tantrum continued. His father yelled at him to stop it. He threatened a spanking. He threatened no more TV. He yelled until he was hoarse, not caring that Marjorie heard. He would show her how to handle this situation! He closed the bathroom door to wait out the tantrum. He looked at his watch. It was quarter to eight. Stephen was exhausted. He decided to skip baths. He picked up Adam and took him into his room. Jeremy was already in his room, having changed into his pajamas himself. For once Stephen felt immensely grateful that his older son was so good.

"Okay, we're going to put on our pajamas," Stephen said.

"No," Adam said.

This child was too contrary. He was definitely out for trouble. "You're looking for it," Stephen said. "You're doing this on purpose." He must be mad at me because Marjorie isn't here, spoiling him as usual, he thought.

"No pajamas," Adam said.

"You're going to wear them whether you like to or not," Stephen said, and with that he grabbed at Adam's jogging suit, which he was still wearing from that day and the night before. Adam began to howl.

"Mommy lets him sleep in his clothes," Jeremy said from the doorway.

"I do *not* want to hear what Mommy does!" Stephen yelled. "I'll handle this my way!" Jeremy burst into tears and went back to his room.

Stephen tried to pull the clothes off Adam's twisting, kicking body. Stephen had no idea where Adam got such strength, why he wasn't tired and ready for bed after so many emotional scenes and tantrums.

After several minutes of struggling, Stephen had succeeded in getting off Adam's pants, but not his sweat shirt. He decided to leave it alone for now. "Okay," he said, panting, "it's time for bed."

"Mommy," Adam cried.

"She'll be here in a minute." It had been Stephen's fantasy that he would have Adam, all scrubbed and bathed and quiet, lying in his fresh pajamas all tucked in and ready to sleep. But how could he let Marjorie see the shambles they had made of Adam's bed and room as they had fought? And Adam's face was dirty and tear-streaked. Stephen wasn't doing a very good job of getting his kid to bed. He didn't even know where Jeremy had gone or what he should do about him. Adam was enough trouble for one night.

"Okay, Adam. Now we're going to sleep. I'm going to put out the light."

"No!" Adam shrieked.

"Yes, I am," he said. "It's late and time for you to sleep."

"I'm not tired. I want to watch TV."

"No more TV," Stephen said. "Bedtime."

Adam began to howl.

"All right, you can stay up, but only in your room and only for a few minutes."

Adam stopped howling and got up to play with his toys, which were scattered across the floor.

Stephen, exhausted, went downstairs to get a drink. He did not know what to do anymore.

He lowered himself into an armchair and closed his eyes. Later, when he felt better, he would apologize to Marjorie. Things were quite a bit different from what he'd imagined. He didn't know how she handled this every day. He had never dreamed that Adam could be so difficult.

◆

Adam's family is a composite, based on the experiences of several families with extremely difficult children. Adam is highly active, intense, poorly adaptable, highly persistent, distractible and irregular; he has a low threshold, and withdraws in new situations. He is also, when not angry or miserable, a child whose basic disposition is quite sunny, who can enjoy things, who has creative ability in the area of art, and who could become, if properly handled, an interesting, energetic, and enthusiastic older child. But this is a family in trouble. Both parents are at a loss for answers, and it's clear that something—or someone—is going to give. Who will it be: Adam, his mother, his father, his older brother—or the marriage? And this day is just one of many, with its assortment of crises and confrontations. Some days are better and some worse. But no day passes without Adam affecting its rhythms and its activities. The family stands, perpetually, in the shadow of this child.

✦

As you prepare to devise a program for your difficult child, remember again a few basic principles.

• The term "difficult" is relative. How difficult is *your child in your particular family*? The concept of fit is very important here.
• Difficult children are not all alike. Your child may be quite different from Adam in some ways. What makes *your* child difficult will depend on his particular combination of difficult traits.
• The degree of change you will need to make in dealing with your child will depend not only on how difficult he is, but also on how long an established vicious circle has existed in your family.

Let us begin now the comprehensive study of your individual child.

PART II

A PROGRAM FOR YOUR DIFFICULT CHILD

INTRODUCTION

You are about to undertake a program that, with your consistent application, will enable you to improve your child's and family's situation. Many of the principles and techniques you will learn are incorporated in the Difficult Child Program that I established at Beth Israel Hospital and are used at the Difficult Child Center in my private practice in New York City.

My philosophy is based on the belief that most parents can significantly alter their attitudes and behavior through *education*. If you can learn to understand your child's difficult temperament, you can begin to correct what is going on with him and with your family.

Gradually you will become an *expert* on your child's temperament and behavior. And since experts can deal with things better, you will, too. You will no longer be so caught up in your own feelings because you will be able to step away and become more objective. Once you have a more neutral point of view, you can become more flexible, more accepting, more authoritative in a positive sense, more of a leader.

Undertaking the program will first change your thinking and ways of reacting. You will then learn certain principles and techniques for managing your child.

THE FIVE ELEMENTS OF YOUR PROGRAM

Evaluation—Defining the Problem

The first part of the program enables you, as parents, to understand your situation more clearly. You will study

97

your child and focus on important family issues such as the mother's and father's reaction to the child, discipline, and other relevant areas. This evaluation, which you will conduct yourselves in Chapter 6, will provide you with the basis for decision-making about your child. It will give you a comprehensive picture of your particular family situation.

Regaining Adult Authority

To restore you to your rightful place of leadership in your family, you need to learn new ways to assert adult authority. Chapter 7 outlines the principles of clear, effective discipline. You will gradually reeducate yourselves to *think temperament and to deal with behavior* instead of responding emotionally or instinctively to what you perceive as the child's motives. You will find that you punish much less, but when you do, you will get results.

You will learn:

- to disengage, to stand back
- to become neutral in your attitude
- to think and evaluate before you respond
- to come to understand your child's puzzling behavior feature by feature as you learn to relate it to his difficult temperament
- to replace "Why is he doing this to me?" with "How can I understand his behavior?"

As you become more and more of an expert on your child, your negative involvement with him and your participation in the vicious circle will be replaced by an *adult attitude* that stresses assertiveness, kindness, brevity, firmness, clear limits, and consistency.

Management Techniques

Once you and your spouse have regained your position as the adults in charge, you now combine your new parental attitude with a variety of management tech-

niques geared to the underlying temperamental issues
in many of the conflicts, problems, and questions that
arise daily with a difficult child. Management, as I use
the term, is very different from punishment. It's more
sympathetic, and it applies to the child's behavior when
"he can't help himself." The message you'll be giving
your child is, "I *understand* you." The techniques can
improve many troublesome temperament-related behaviors that cannot be controlled by discipline or punishment alone. This material is covered in Chapter 8.

In Chapter 9, "Putting It All Together," you'll learn
how to combine your management techniques with your
new approach to discipline to deal successfully with your
child in a variety of day-to-day situations.

In the case of infants, punishment shouldn't even be
an issue. All you can really do is try to understand the
behavior and manage it as best you can. You cannot
change your infant to make him or her an "easy baby."
But recognizing your baby's temperament and learning
to manage it through the suggestions in Chapter 10 can
make your days and nights much less stressful.

Family Guidance

Many problems can arise from the ripple effect caused
by a difficult child. Some of them will be solved by the
application of the program's management techniques,
while others will require further attention. Chapter 11,
"Beyond the Child," contains suggestions concerning aspects of your family life where you need extra support.
These include relations with parents, siblings, extended
family, and peers, and special sections on schools and
pediatricians.

If you think your child or your family might need
more specialized, professional help, this chapter also
provides guidelines on when to seek it and on selecting
the right professionals to consult.

Support Groups

The last aspect of the program includes advice on how to set up a parents' or mothers' support group, including suggestions for what to discuss during meetings, how to contact parents of other difficult children, and how to run such a group yourself. You'll learn the value of hot lines to other mothers as well as how to help handle your feelings of isolation and alienation. Support groups can be organized with or without the aid of professionals; you'll learn how to do this effectively wherever you live. All of this is explained in Chapter 11.

The program attempts to deal comprehensively with all issues related to raising difficult children. Not every family will need every aspect of the program. For example, the parents of a basically easy child with some difficult traits may simply need to change some of their attitudes and learn some management techniques. But before you decide what parts do or do not apply to your particular situation, I urge you to read all of Chapters 6 to 11 in sequence and without skipping.

6

EVALUATING YOUR SITUATION
The Five-Day Study Period

When parents of difficult children first come to see me, I can usually make some assumptions: They are having trouble raising their child, they feel frustrated, and they have lost at least some of their parental authority. If their child is very difficult, they are also confused, often guilty and ashamed, their marriage is being affected, and they feel they and their child are "different."

But while these generalizations usually apply, there are just as many differences. Difficult children, as you already know, are not alike in every respect, and neither are their families. Once I understand the issues for any particular child and his family, I can then make recommendations specific to their situation. Of course I cannot do this in your case, but I can show you how to do *your own* evaluation of your child and family. The aim is to make you, the parents, the experts on your child.

Before embarking on your evaluation, it is best that both of you read this book cover to cover. Significant improvement can sometimes occur without the father's direct involvement. In my experience, however, the chances of success are greatly enhanced if both parents participate actively. A tip for mothers: If your husband is reluctant to read the entire book, insist that he, at the very least, read Chapter 1 and Chapters 6–11.

The Five-Day Study Period

You begin this process over the next five days. If you can't start right away, mark a block of five days on your

calendar and reserve them for this purpose. Set aside a
weekend and combine this, if at all possible, with a few
days off from work. During these five days your main
objective is to familiarize yourselves thoroughly with
your child's behavior and his temperament, and the link
between the two in a variety of everyday situations. You
will also be looking at yourselves, your responses to the
child, and the general family situation.

During this time you should:

• *Simplify your life.* Don't make a lot of social
engagements, don't take the child on unnecessary
errands, make your daily routine as easy as possible
for yourself.

• *Schedule lots of time together for parental
discussions.* This is really important. The process of
working on your evaluation should be one of give-
and-take. Discuss everything, and try to find answers that reflect the way both of you feel.

• *In a special notebook, try to record your answers to the questionnaires that follow.* I know that
some parents will regard this as an unnecessary
chore, but writing things down will clarify your
thinking, and your written evaluation will prove
useful later, when you are learning new ways of
disciplining and new management techniques. It will
also serve as a concrete measure of progress as your
situation begins to improve.

• *Most importantly, back away from excessive
and ineffective punishments.* Try to stop most threats,
yelling, screaming, and spankings while you are
studying the situation. Just note in your book what
has occurred. And remember to make the limited
punishment you do mete out very brief.

This is a very difficult time for many parents because they become concerned that they are "giving in,"
that the child will take advantage, and that they will
lose the last vestige of authority.

Be sure you remember the goal. You are studying a
new way of thinking and a new method of response.

Before you can apply something new, you have to stop what you have been doing. To unlearn an established pattern, even an ineffective one, is difficult and takes time.

A BEHAVIORAL PROFILE OF YOUR CHILD

Look first at the *types* of behavior that cause problems in your family, the things your child does that give you the most trouble. Here is a list of common types of problem behavior, together with some of the alternate ways parents have described them to me. Use these categories as a guide to making your own list in your notebook.

Which of these behaviors does your child display?

TYPE OF BEHAVIOR	PARENTS' DESCRIPTIONS
Defiant	—Does whatever he wants —Ignores what I say —Does exactly the opposite of what I tell him
Resistive	—Refuses to listen —Won't follow directions —Dawdles —Always finds excuses
Inattentive	—Doesn't "listen" —Tunes out —Daydreams
Stubborn	—Has to get his own way —Won't take no for an answer —Incredibly strong-willed
Shy	—Very timid —Clings to my skirts —Always hides her face —Holds back
Particular	—Very picky —Faddy —Only wants certain things —Really hard to please —Fussy, always noticing little things no one else does

TYPE OF BEHAVIOR	PARENTS' DESCRIPTIONS
Complaining	−Whines a lot −Pouts −Sulks −Never satisfied
Interrupting	−Breaks into adult conversations −Won't let me talk on the phone
Intrusive	−Invades my privacy −Comes into our room even when told not to
Verbally angry	−Swears a lot −Calls people names—even grown-ups −Yells
Bad manners	−Horrible at the table −Sassy, fresh to me, always talks back −Takes toys away from other children −Rude
Selfish	−Won't share toys with siblings or friends −Everything is "mine!"
Wild behavior	−Gets overexcited −Gets revved up easily −Creates a disturbance −Can be destructive; throws or breaks things
Impulsive	−Loses control −Has outbursts over small things −Can't seem to stop himself
Physically aggressive	−Pushes and shoves people −Hits, kicks, or bites other children or even adults
Temper tantrums	−May vary in intensity and duration

The next step is to put together your child's *type of behavior* with the *situations or settings* in which it occurs. This is important because I want you to see how the same behavior can manifest itself in quite different areas. For example, a child who is "resistive" can exhibit this when getting dressed (by dawdling), in school (by finding excuses), and at mealtimes (by ignoring your comments about table manners). Feel free to include in your list any other situations and settings that apply in your case.

- Getting up in the morning
- Getting dressed, clothing
- Mealtimes and food
- Bedtime and sleep
- Watching TV
- Playing
- Family activities
- Interactions with siblings
- Interactions with peers
- Interactions with housekeeper
- School and teachers
- Public places

To show you how your finished behavioral profile will look, here is a sample completed by the parents of a very difficult child named Janie:

A BEHAVIORAL PROFILE OF JANIE, AGE 4

TYPE OF BEHAVIOR	SITUATION OR SETTING
Resistive	–Getting up in the morning –Getting dressed, clothing –Bedtime and sleep –Mealtimes and food
Stubborn	–Getting dressed, clothing –Mealtimes and food –School and teachers
Particular	–Clothing and food
Shy	–School and teachers –Public places

TYPE OF BEHAVIOR	SITUATION OR SETTING
Complaining	–Getting up in the morning –Getting dressed, clothing –Mealtimes and food –Bedtime and sleep –Family activities –Interactions with siblings –Public places
Selfish	–Watching TV –Family activities –Interactions with peers –Interactions with siblings –School
Temper tantrums	–Getting dressed, clothing –Public places

This behavioral profile is very useful, because it will help you begin to sort out your confused impressions and see that there is some inner pattern and coherence in your child's problem behavior. His responses in school may in fact be closely related to his reaction when you try to dress him. Thus one type of behavior may be causing trouble in more than one setting.

A TEMPERAMENTAL PROFILE OF YOUR CHILD

In learning to deal with your child, half the battle is to recognize the temperamental issues that often cause problem behavior. Later you'll learn that when you find a temperamental issue underlying the behavior, you'll *manage* your child rather than *punishing* him.

Now you're going to draw up a temperamental profile of your child. Draw your information from the following list of difficult traits. Ask yourself questions about your child's temperament in each of the areas. Is he very active? Is he irregular? Is he intense (loud)? You are trying to pinpoint *how* difficult your child is in each area. Remember, the question is not whether he is very difficult overall, but rather whether he is very difficult, moderately difficult, or mildly difficult in this *one* area.

To show you how this might look, I've followed your blank temperamental profile with a sample profile of Janie.

DIFFICULT TRAITS

High Activity Level
Very active, restless, fidgety; always into things; makes you tired; "ran before he walked"; easily overstimulated; gets wild or "revved up"; impulsive, loses control, can be aggressive; hates to be confined.

Distractibilty
Has trouble concentrating and paying attention, especially if not really interested; doesn't "listen"; tunes you out; daydreams; forgets instructions.

High Intensity
Loud and forceful whether miserable, angry, or happy.

Irregularity
Unpredictable. Can't tell when he'll be hungry or tired; conflict over meals and bedtime; wakes up at night; moods are changeable; has good or bad days for no obvious reason.

Negative Persistence
Stubborn; goes on and on nagging, whining, or negotiating if wants something; relentless, won't give up; gets "locked in"; may have long tantrums.

Low Sensory Threshold
"Sensitive"—physically not emotionally; highly aware of color, light, appearance, texture, sound, smell, taste, or temperature (not necessarily all of these); "creative" but with strong and unusual preferences which can be embarrassing; clothes have to feel and look right, making dressing a problem; doesn't like the way many foods look, smell, or taste; picky eater; bothered and overstimulated by bright lights and noisy settings; refuses to dress warmly when the weather is cold.

Initial Withdrawal
Shy and reserved with new people; doesn't like new situations; holds back or protests by crying or clinging; may tantrum if forced to go forward.

Poor Adaptability
Has trouble with transition and change—of activity or routine; inflexible, very particular, notices minor changes; gets used to things and won't give them up; has trouble adapting to anything unfamiliar; can want the same clothes or foods over and over.

Negative Mood
Basically serious or cranky; doesn't show pleasure openly; not a "sunny" disposition.

YOUR CHILD

	VERY DIFFICULT	MODERATELY DIFFICULT	MILDLY DIFFICULT
Activity level	☐	☐	☐
Distractibility	☐	☐	☐
Intensity	☐	☐	☐
Regularity	☐	☐	☐
Negative Persistence	☐	☐	☐
Sensory threshold	☐	☐	☐
Approach/withdrawal	☐	☐	☐
Adaptability	☐	☐	☐
Mood	☐	☐	☐

A TEMPERAMENTAL PROFILE OF JANIE, AGE 4

	VERY DIFFICULT	MODERATELY DIFFICULT	MILDLY DIFFICULT
Activity level	☐	☐	☐
Distractibility	☐	☐	☐
Intensity	☐	☑	☐

	VERY DIFFICULT	MODERATELY DIFFICULT	MILDLY DIFFICULT
Regularity	☐	☑	☐
Negative persistence	☑	☐	☐
Sensory threshold	☑	☐	☐
Approach/withdrawal	☐	☑	☐
Adaptability	☑	☐	☐
Mood	☑	☐	☐

RELATING BEHAVIOR TO TEMPERAMENT

Any time you can link your child's behavior to a difficult temperamental trait, the behavior immediately becomes less puzzling. Go back now to your child's behavioral profile. Review each type of behavior and the setting in which it occurs. Ask yourself: "Can I possibly relate this behavior to my child's temperament?" Any time you see such a connection, put a "T" next to the behavior. Do this even if the linkage is not 100 percent clear. For example, complaining behavior may sometimes clearly relate to poor adaptability (when a transition is involved), but at other times may be manipulative in nature. In such instances, still put a "T" next to the behavior, but make a mental note.

To illustrate, let us link Janie's behavior to her temperament:

Her resistive, stubborn behavior is often evident when she is getting dressed. She insists on wearing the same old jeans. She doesn't like certain clothes or says they feel wrong. This is due to poor adaptability and negative persistence, plus a low threshold to the way clothes feel. If the issue of dressing becomes a problem, and her mother insists that Janie wear certain clothes, a temper tantrum may result.

Bedtime troubles are due to her irregular sleep patterns, which have been evident since infancy. Her parents try to make her go to sleep; the child is not tired at the same time every night; going to bed thus becomes a nightly struggle; and a complex vicious circle has evolved.

Particular and stubborn behavior at mealtimes can be attributed to a combination of poor adaptability, a low threshold to the taste and smell of food, and irregular appetite rhythms.

Janie's generally selfish attitude, which manifests itself with TV-watching (she wants to see only *her* shows), interactions with her playmates and siblings, and behavior at school and during family activities, can be linked to her negative persistence and poor adaptability. She gets "locked in" to what she's doing and doesn't want to change.

Her shyness, manifested as clinging and holding back with strangers and in public places, can be due to her initial withdrawal, plus her generally low threshold, which results in her getting overstimulated. Too much of this also can lead to a tantrum.

In school much of her problem behavior is related to her difficulty with transitions, with changes in routine, and with sharing. This again is due to her poor adaptability and persistence.

And finally, Janie's generally complaining, seemingly "unhappy" demeanor is partly due to her negative mood.

Please note that her parents did not give Janie a rating in two areas—activity level and distractibility—because neither is a problem with this child.

As you review your child's temperamental profile, you may be surprised to see how many problem behaviors you have been able to relate, directly or indirectly, to your child's inborn temperamental features. This information is crucial to the success of your program, and you will be coming back to it over and over again in the weeks to come.

FAMILY ISSUES

In Part I of this book, you were introduced to the vicious circle and to the ways in which the family is affected by the difficult child. I'd like you now to look at your own situation and see how *your* family is being affected. It's particularly important for you to do this as a couple. You don't need to make a list, but there should be lots of discussion. Try to see things from everyone's point of view.

---

1. *How is the mother affected?*
   This includes such issues as exhaustion, bewilderment, a sense of isolation and inadequacy, feeling ostracized and "different," guilt, and anger.

2. *How is the father affected?*
   Do you feel excluded from the mother/child relationship? Do you feel your wife is doing a "bad job" as a mother? Are you also angry, guilty, or exhausted?

3. *How are the siblings affected?*
   This includes such areas as siblings being "too good" to contrast with the difficult child, being "bad" to get attention, feeling neglected, or becoming withdrawn.

4. *How is the marriage affected?*
   Do you feel you have no time for each other? Do you fight a lot about how to handle the child? Are you always blaming each other? Is your relationship generally suffering?

5. *How is your relationship with your extended family affected?*
   This includes relations with parents, in-laws, and your brothers and sisters. Does your family criticize you a lot about how you're raising your child? Are get-togethers affected adversely? Do you argue with your mother or mother-in-law (or both) a lot about the child?

6. *Are other family problems worsening?*
   Drinking problems, money worries, a parent's tendency to depression, and other problems can be exacerbated.

Please don't use your discussion to rub salt in old wounds, blame each other, or open arguments anew. Listen, instead, for *new* information about how the members of your family are feeling and reacting. *All* families with difficult children are affected to some degree.

WEAR AND TEAR

Once you know how the vicious circle affects you and your family, it's time to look at how it affects your difficult child. He, too, may suffer secondary problems as a result of the tension and friction. Ask yourself if your child:

	YES	NO
Seems angry a lot	☐	☐
Clings (even when no initial withdrawal is involved)	☐	☐
Is fearful a lot	☐	☐
Has frequent bad dreams	☐	☐
Is oversensitive and easily upset	☐	☐
Doesn't seem to like himself	☐	☐
Says things like "I'm bad"	☐	☐

Many of these problems may abate as you apply the principles of the program. You will also learn some sympathetic approaches specifically to deal with wear-and-tear behavior. Later, if these problems persist in spite of the improved family atmosphere, you may need further help for your child.

IS YOUR DISCIPLINE EFFECTIVE?

Ineffective discipline is one of the biggest problems in a family with a difficult child. Try to answer these questions honestly. They are not meant to make you feel inadequate, but rather to focus your attention on "methods" that simply do not work with a difficult child. "Yeses" on the questionnaire indicate ineffective techniques and frustrations that you *do not have to live with*. The answer, surprisingly, is not *more* punishment but *less*—as you will see in the next chapter.

	YES	NO
Do you find yourself screaming and yelling a lot?	☐	☐
Do you descend to the child's level? (e.g., if he hits you, do you hit him back?)	☐	☐
Do you punish the child far more than you want to?	☐	☐
Are you always saying "no" to the child?	☐	☐
Do you feel you have to repeat yourself all the time?	☐	☐
Are you battling your child a lot?	☐	☐
Are you constantly explaining to your child?	☐	☐
Are you always negotiating with him?	☐	☐
Are you often getting him to promise he'll never do it again?	☐	☐
Are you threatening things you really don't intend to carry out?	☐	☐
Do you overreact with a major punishment to something you realize later is relatively minor?	☐	☐
In between the punishments do you overcompensate by "spoiling" the child?	☐	☐
Do you and your husband react very differently to the same behavior?	☐	☐
Do you sometimes not know how to respond?	☐	☐
Does the child seem more powerful than you?	☐	☐

Do you find the more you punish the child, the more he does what he's not supposed to do?	☐	☐
Do you nag him all the time?	☐	☐
Are you frequently changing your mind about your methods of punishment?	☐	☐
Do you give in a lot?	☐	☐

Now think about ways of handling your child's behavior that *have* worked. Have you ever tried something spontaneously—even something you didn't think of as "discipline"—and been almost surprised at how quickly your child responded? Is there *one* punishment that seems to carry special weight with your child? Recognizing and recording your successes, even if they seem relatively few, will help you later in finding creative solutions for your child and family.

THE "RELEVANT BEHAVIOR" LIST

One of the main reasons for ineffective discipline with a difficult child is that the parents are so caught up, so irritated by the child that they respond to virtually *anything* he does. And the more they overreact the more the child misbehaves. In a sense, the child continues to get even more attention paid to him. Excessive attention, even if it's negative, is such a powerful "reward" to a child that it actually *reinforces* the undesirable behavior. You need to learn restraint, to respond to far fewer situations, to ask yourself questions like, "Is this really important?" "Could I let this behavior go?" "What would happen if I just wait?" "Could I lose by doing nothing?"

To help you to react less, one final list is needed. When I consult with a family I ask the mother and the father to draw up separate lists of the behaviors of their child that are *truly* unacceptable. This is called "relevant behavior," *the behavior that objectively speaking you as a parent feel you have to take a stand on and change*. Make sure that when you focus on each behavior you ask yourself what you realistically can expect. For example, though sitting quietly through a meal may be important to you, are you overreacting to your child's behavior at the table? Maybe you could let some things go. Try to put only *really important* things on your "relevant behavior" list.

Once you have made your list and ascertained that the behaviors on it are really objectively relevant (go back over your list and ask yourself one more time if each item is), switch lists with your partner. The lists will, most likely, be somewhat different. You should then begin to negotiate with each other toward the goal of one list of behaviors relevant to both of you. And in your negotiations, you should strive once again to base your conclusions on objectivity and not merely irritation. For example, many mothers get very locked into power struggles over what their child wears, or eats for breakfast. They say things like, "She doesn't listen to what's good for her, she always wants her own way." Everything becomes an issue; the child's demand for potato chips each morning instead of a bowl of cereal takes on crisis proportions. The mother becomes overly concerned about nutrition. She worries about the future. She vacillates between getting angry and giving in. But for now, unless the pediatrician is concerned about the child's nutritional state, the mother should try to view such behavior as irrelevant. Later, when the general family atmosphere improves, she can always come back to the potato chips. Another extremely irritating behavior with these children is swearing or name-calling. Many difficult children will call their parents "stupid" or worse. Understandably the parents are very upset by this. Right now, for the purposes of your list, try to treat this as irrelevant. Again, *you can come back to it later*. Most likely there are more immediately important issues, and these are the ones you should focus on now.

Here are some guidelines to help you narrow that focus:

1. List no motivations, just behaviors. Concentrate on the fact that your child won't change her clothes, not that she won't change her clothes *because* "she always wants her own way."

2. Is this *important*? Get away from mere irritation. Is it really important that he bangs his toys loudly? Or is it more important that he hits his siblings with these toys as well?

3. Is the item important to *both* parents? Your final list must be consistent, because both of you will take a stand on these behaviors.

4. Are you being *objective*? Step back from the list (and the child) and aim for a rational assessment of the behavior. Don't make your lists when the child is around. Make them at a time when both of you are calm. Sit down in a quiet room with no distractions, such as television. And do this when you have enough time for discussion rather than writing things down haphazardly and calling it "done."

5. How extensive is the behavior in *degree*? Does it occur every night, for instance, or only once in a while?

6. Do not concern yourself with projections into the future. Handle the *now*. Your child's personality when he grows up is not at issue ("What will become of him if I allow him to use bad words/have bad table manners/refuse to say hello when he is introduced to someone? I'm afraid he'll turn out wrong.").

This process of sorting and negotiating a mutually agreeable list of *really* relevant behaviors is not easy. Don't get discouraged if it doesn't seem to come out right immediately. You may have to spend more time sorting things out than you imagined. But I can't emphasize enough how important this process is, because your list will become the foundation of your effective discipline, and the concept of relevant vs. irrelevant behavior will be utilized in every situation that calls for parental authority.

Enter your final list in your notebook under the heading, "Relevant Behavior."

One final note: Don't be afraid to change or refine

your list. Something new and important may occur to you that should be included. Or you may decide to remove an item.

To aid you in this job, let's look at the lists made by a hypothetical couple, Susan and Douglas, whose 3½-year-old son Robby is a classically difficult child. When they have finished with their first attempt, this is what they have set down:

MOTHER'S LIST	FATHER'S LIST
Eats too many hot dogs	Sulks, always in a bad mood
Bites other children	Doesn't appreciate presents
Won't share toys	Touches all my things
Has long tantrums	Won't listen to me
Purposely breaks things	Behaves badly with strangers
Won't wear anything new	Watches too much TV
Terrible table manners	Comes into our bed at night
Yells and screams loudly when bathed	Cries too much
Always wants his own way	Bites children
Can't take him anywhere	Bad tantrums

They now exchange lists and begin their discussion. Douglas immediately says, "Why are you so bothered by his eating hot dogs?" Susan explains that she often gives their child hot dogs for lunch, because he likes them and it's easier than fixing something more complicated that he generally refuses. She worries she may be doing him harm. But after some discussion, they realize the hot dog issue isn't that important; their son is generally healthy. Their pediatrician has even told them to relax about his eating habits. Hot dogs go off the list. Susan notices the entry on Doug's list "Comes into our bed at night." She doesn't mind this, she tells her husband. "I think it's our room and we should have privacy," he says. Susan is protective and worries about Robby's night fears. Doug insists that they need to be alone. They leave this on their relevant list, after much discussion. They question table manners because when they compare this to biting and temper tantrums, it seems much less important. They decide to leave in throwing food but discard the more minor examples of poor manners. Susan points out that Doug's entry "Won't listen to me" is not specific enough and should be modified. He points out that *purposely* breaking things raises the question of motivation. He feels that most of the time it's accidental. They both decide that they should keep more things out of Robby's reach and watch him more carefully when he's revved up. They also agree that yelling during a bath is really not so bad. After more talk, their relevant list looks like this:

> Has severe, long tantrums
> Bites other children
> Can't take him anywhere
> Throws food at the table.
> Won't wear anything new
> Doesn't obey
> Sulks, always in a bad mood
> Comes into our bed at night
> Cries too much

This isn't a bad job for a relevant behavior list, but it could use some refining. The parents refer back to the temperamental profile on Robby. "Won't wear anything new" is an item related to temperament. This child has a low sensory threshold and is sensitive to the feel of new clothes. He is also poorly adaptable. He doesn't like "new" things because he doesn't like change. But when you analyze this more closely, although you discover it really bothers both parents, you will also find that it can be sidestepped. New clothes could be washed and made softer. His parents could buy new things just like the articles of clothing the child already likes, and avoid some of the conflict. Or they could ignore this problem for now and try not to care so deeply what Robby wears. "Sulks, always in a bad mood," may also be an expression of the child's temperament (negative mood); but even if this is not totally true, it is not the kind of behavior that should be punished. Temperament-related

problems can often be handled in a special way, as you
will see in Chapter 8.

Be as specific as possible about your child's behavior. Susan writes "Can't take him anywhere," but this is
an expression of her exasperation rather than a description of the behavior she finds objectionable. Is Robby
hard to take places because he tantrums, whines, clings,
or runs wild? Are there temperamental issues involved?
When and where does Robby's crying seem excessive
and out of place? Are there particular situations that set
him off? And what about, "Doesn't obey"? Perhaps Susan and Doug expect obedience in too many situations.
They should define more clearly specific and limited
instances of disobedience.

What you want to end up with on your list are
at most five or six behaviors that you both agree have
to be changed. They might include such behaviors as
tantrums; physically aggressive behavior to an excess
(biting fits in here); undue intrusion into parental
privacy (sleeping in parents' bed); wild behavior in
public (runs away and grabs in the supermarket); interrupting adult conversations; refusing to get dressed in
the morning; throwing food. In general, your final relevant behavior list should consist of behaviors that are
both truly unacceptable and, that you both agree, can be
controlled by your child—at least to some extent.

A Final Word

What you now know about your situation is:

- the kinds of behavior that trouble you
- where those behaviors occur
- the underlying temperamental issues related
to some of the behaviors
- whether your family is being affected by the
strain of the vicious circle
- whether your child is showing signs of wear
and tear
- how ineffective your discipline may be

• the behaviors that are *truly relevant*—those that both parents should *always* take a stand on

And now you are going to learn what to do about all of this.

7

REGAINING ADULT AUTHORITY
Discipline That Works

My initial task when I see a family is to convince parents to give up the way they have been "disciplining" their child. Even though they know their old way isn't working, they find it frightening to start all over again.

The "authority" they have been trying to assert is mostly ineffective: saying "no" much more often than necessary, getting caught up in repeated power struggles, sinking to the level of the child, and doing a great deal of yelling and threatening.

The goal of this chapter is to help you replace ineffective discipline with a benign, firm, practical, adult attitude. You will find that you punish much less, but that when you do, it will be effective.

Try to remember always the golden principle: *The more authority you have, the less you will need to punish.*

There are two components to an effective disciplinary system with a young child—Planned Actions and Reactions.

Planned actions are the various decisions arrived at by the parents regarding rules, routines, expectations, and consequences. These are shared with the child in calm discussions which always take place *away* from the heat of the moment.

Reactions are on-the-spot responses to unacceptable behavior. Punishment is one example of a reaction.

The information you have compiled on your child and family situation in the course of the five-day study period forms the basis for what you are about to undertake in this chapter.

121

PLANNED ACTIONS

In order to restore you to your rightful parental roles as the leaders in your family, an overall approach—a strategy—has to be devised for dealing with your difficult child. If the child is particularly hard to raise you are no doubt in the unfortunate situation where "the tail is wagging the dog." To reverse this aspect of the vicious circle you need to plan carefully. At least 75 percent of effective discipline comes about when the parents have calmly and rationally arrived at decisions *away* from the "trench warfare" of day-to-day life with a very difficult child.

I cannot emphasize enough the importance of these strategic discussions. Hold them when the children are in bed or when the two of you are out of the house. Try to aim for some kind of an agenda and a problem-solving attitude, and don't allow your discussions to degenerate into "woe-is-me" complaining sessions.

The Importance of Rules

As you arrive at a clearer mutual definition of rules, expectations, and consequences, make sure that your child is informed. Too often we assume that our children know what is expected of them. But it is *not* true that a child knows what you want simply because there has been a lot of yelling and threatening. He will do much better if you inform him of your decisions *away from the heat of the moment*. Define what you intend to tell him, make sure both parents are in agreement, and sit down with him when everything is calm. Be friendly but firm, and say something like this: "Your mother and I have been thinking about your throwing food at the table. The new rule in our house is that this is not allowed. Please try your best, but if you can't control yourself you'll have to finish your meal by yourself in the kitchen." You may have told your child this before, but never in this coherent, calm, and firm manner, and, almost certainly, never *away* from the actual incident.

In these kinds of planned discussions children are

not only informed of new rules and expectations, but also kindly and firmly encouraged to do their best. I believe very strongly that young children, including the difficult ones, would much rather please their parents than battle them. In approaching them in this way we make it easier for them to follow their natural inclinations. And, of course, when the child does achieve some success, it is important to acknowledge his efforts—not by raving ecstatically about every minor accomplishment —but by lovingly letting him know that you've noticed that he is trying harder and you are proud of him.

What rules should you establish? Obviously this is dependent on each individual family situation. I don't believe in imposing a "right way" on families. For example, how much TV your child watches is up to you as parents, and is not something I generally address. However, there is one "rule" that I do recommend. Make sure there is a clear definition of privacy in your home. In many families the children have unlimited access to the parents—they are allowed to intrude into adult conversations, into the parents' bedroom, even into the bathroom. This is surely wrong. Especially in a family where a difficult child is too dominant, some clear rules regarding privacy need to be established. As a parent you are entitled to go into your bedroom, or at the very least into the bathroom, close the door, and be alone. Conversely, depending on your child's age, he too is entitled to privacy. For example, you don't need to be present when your 4-year-old uses the toilet.

Structure and Routines

In our modern society many parents are very aware of the need to prepare their children for a complex future. An early start to formal education is becoming the norm. Television frequently portrays children as miniature adults. I often see 4-year-olds who behave as if they were eight, and 10-year-olds who could pass for teenagers.

In our well-intentioned efforts to stimulate our youngsters intellectually we can easily forget that emotionally they are still young children. The resulting lack of discipline and structure is not in the best interest of most children, and most certainly not good for the difficult ones, where an inevitable by-product of the vicious circle is that the child is viewed as too powerful and the parents have lost some or most of their authority.

Structure, a very important component of effective discipline, refers to a clear and consistent emphasis on predictability. Difficult children invariably do better if they know what is expected of them, *provided the expectations don't change constantly.* Many events and activities in the day-to-day life of the child can be made more structured—bedtime, meals, watching television, and bathing are just a few examples. Any time you have a situation which is erratic and emotionally charged, you will almost certainly improve it by introducing some structure. And the way to inform your child, as you have already seen, is *not* in the middle of an unpleasant situation, but in the course of a calm, planned discussion.

Your own behavior might also benefit from this emphasis. Take, for example, a working woman in a pressured job who works late most days. Whenever possible she comes guiltily rushing home at two o'clock to spend some time with her child. Such a mother, and her child, might be much better off if she planned to be home, predictably, at four o'clock on the same two days each week. And many parents find that the family atmosphere improves if the father makes a point of getting home in time for a proper family dinner several times during the week.

Structure is not the same as rigidity. As a matter of fact, structure and flexibility go hand-in-hand, just as firmness and kindness do. You can insist that your child be dressed for school at a certain time each day, but let her choose her clothes (even if the color combinations make you gulp in dismay). You can enforce a bedtime during the week, but be more flexible over weekends and vacations. The child can have a regular Sunday "father and son" outing with his daddy, but he can help decide what they will do.

A **routine** is a predictable sequence of prescribed events, occurring in the same order every day. Most difficult children thrive on routines. Here is a real opportunity to recruit your child's *positive* persistence. The same temperamental quality that can make your little girl go on like a broken record when she wants something or that locks her into an activity will work for you once she gets used to a routine, so that it in effect becomes a "good habit." And many overinvolved mothers of difficult children find, to their surprise, that they are far less needed than they could have imagined once a routine is established.

In many homes, the two most important routines to be established are the morning routine and the evening routine. Here are some sample routines:

MORNING	EVENING (begin after dinner)
Get up	Family play
Go to bathroom (wash face, brush teeth, etc.)	Watch TV
	Go to bathroom
Get dressed	Change for bed
Eat breakfast	Story
Watch TV	Bedtime
Leave for school	

It is permissible to be flexible about the hours at which these events take place or how long each part takes (for example, the time the child watches TV at night may vary), but the *sequence* must remain the same. He always goes to the bathroom right after TV, then changes for bed. In the *same order*. You can let the child help decide on the sequence of events. Ask him if he likes to change into his pajamas before brushing his teeth at night or the other way around. Give the child a sense of mastery and participation.

Then, when the list has been selected, draw up a chart on which this sequence is printed. Be clever and creative. Make the chart attractive. From magazines you can cut pictures of the different activities (e.g., one of a child eating breakfast to accompany that event). Make this fun, and involve your child in it.

Next, pick a specific day, perhaps a Monday, to get

started. Don't introduce various aspects of the routine piecemeal, but rather start all of it on the same day. The first few times the child goes through his routine you can be present to supervise, but after that you should let him do it on his own. Remember, it's *the child's routine* not yours. Fathers can be of help here by encouraging overzealous mothers to hold back.

One final tip: If you include TV in the morning routine, make sure it's *last* on the list, just before school. Let your child know that he has to complete all the other steps before he can watch TV.

PLANNED REWARDS

Many parents feel that they need more effective punishments to respond to the frequent misbehavior of their difficult child. But is there any way to improve your child's behavior *without* punishing him? How can you get your child to listen to you, to abide by the rules of your home? Many if not most parents of difficult children complain to me that they constantly nag, punish, and say "no" and *still* don't get what they want with their kids. Why don't they?

If you stand back and look at the situation objectively, you'll see that you may be in a critical, negative mode with your child. *You*, as well as the child, are locked into what he is doing wrong. Over and over again you are constantly trying to correct it. This doesn't work with any child. And this doesn't work with the difficult child in spades.

How about shifting the mode you are operating in and moving toward an attitude that supports the positive things your child does?

"But," you say, "suppose my child never does anything positive?"

Then let's offer your child inducements to behave positively.

"But that's bribing him," you reply.

No! There's a difference between a bribe and a reward. Bribery is what a parent does to get a kid off her back. The parent is pressured by the behavior, so she

says, "If you'll just stop screaming, I'll buy you a doll."
It's an on-the-spot response in a tense emotional climate.
If repeated over and over it leads to a spoilt kid who
demands something before he'll do anything.

Difficult children may also be spoiled, for another
reason. Their parents feel so guilty that they overcom-
pensate by constantly buying the child presents. The
end result can be a child who is both insecure and
tyrannical—another example of "wear and tear."

Bribery and spoiling are not good for any child,
especially a difficult one, but planned rewards are
another matter entirely.

Think of it this way: When an adult goes to work
or when a teenager baby-sits, they are not being bribed
to do their job. They are earning money. Similarly,
a child can be taught to earn rewards for acceptable
behavior.

The Principles of a Reward System

• Rewards are applied in a *planned way* rather
than as a spot response.

• The mode the parent operates in is neutral.
You are *thinking,* you are not emotional ("Get this
kid off my back!").

• A reward is always given *after* the completion
of the act, *not before.*

• The reward is for *specific behaviors,* not attitudes. Never reward your child for being "good" or
"pleasant."

• The reward itself should also be specific, rather
than a vague promise of a "special treat."

The system works this way: Choose a specific behavior you want the child to carry out. For example: "I've
been dressing you in the morning. If you can dress yourself before you come and watch TV for five mornings,
you'll receive a present." (The goal of five is arbitrary; if
five days are beyond your child's reach, make it smaller.
Set realistic goals and remember that you want your
child to succeed.)

Once you decide what you want the child to do, you and the child discuss the reward. This can be negotiated, to some extent, but keep things in perspective; you don't want to choose a fifty-dollar video game because the child brushes her teeth for two days. Keep your child's interests in mind and bring him into the process of selecting the present.

When a very large task is involved, it's easier to break it down into combinations of behaviors. Let's take keeping the child's room clean. This might seem overwhelming to your child at first, so break down the jobs. Making the bed is one part, putting dolls on the doll shelf the second, putting clothes away the third. Don't be vague about what you want; make it specific so you can judge whether the child is doing it right or wrong. Is she to put away *all* the dolls on the shelf, or *most* of the dolls, or just the small dolls? Your child should clearly understand what is required.

Rewarding for a Routine: The Star System

As already noted, most difficult children do well with routines, especially when large blocks of unplanned time are involved. With some, simply establishing the routine will be enough, but others will need a reward system to help them get started.

This method can be applied to children as young as 3.

If your child completes the routine once, use a mini-reward. This can be a sticker or a star. Help your child pick out colorful stickers or stars and a pretty book or chart to paste them in. For most children the star system alone won't be enough of an inducement. Tell the child he is to get a big reward, a present, when the routine is completed a certain number of times, *but not necessarily in a row*. A rough guide, for example, is to ask a 4-year-old to complete an evening routine five or six times. If the child misses a day you can say, "Bad luck. You didn't earn your star tonight (or this morning), but maybe tomorrow." The present should be decided on by you and the child when you set up the system, but should be left in the store until he's earned the required number of stars.

Use this system until the child's routine is part of family life. Don't worry; when you withdraw the system, the child is unlikely to revert. And if you have a bit of trouble, you can always go back to the system for a short while. The children, however, don't *want* to go back. They like the calmer atmosphere and feel a sense of accomplishment. On the average, the star system for a routine is no longer needed at the end of two months.

Three things to remember:

• Be very clear and specific about the steps in the routine and the exact number of stars needed to earn the present. Go over this a few times.

• You can supervise at first, but this means reminding him once that it's time to move from playing with his blocks to brushing his teeth. It does *not* mean taking over for the child. (If you succeed in holding back, perhaps you too deserve a present.)

• Don't chastise the child if the routine isn't completed. There is no further punishment for an incomplete routine beyond withholding a star.

In summary, the star system works as follows:

1. Choose a *routine* you want to establish.

2. Decide, with the child, on the *sequence of events*. Never vary the sequence.

3. With the child, make an *attractive chart* of the activities.

4. Tell the child that every time he completes the routine he earns a *star* or a *sticker* (he can choose which it is).

5. Every time he accumulates five stars (or whatever other number you decide on), he gets a *reward* (he should participate in choosing the present).

Make it fun, but don't fudge the expectations. He either earns a star or he doesn't. Be sure he knows what he has to do. Remember also that the only "punishment"

in this system is the withholding of the star plus a brief
statement such as, "Bad luck. You didn't earn your star
tonight. Better luck tomorrow."

A final general note: By and large, difficult children
do better with rewards for acceptable behavior than with
punishment for unacceptable behavior. Repeated negative responses to "bad" behavior *reinforce* the behavior
instead of stopping it. And parents like the reward system because it allows them to focus on the child's accomplishments, making parents feel much less guilty.

EFFECTIVE REACTIONS

Punishment is only one part of discipline. Discipline, as
you already know, refers to your general attitude of adult
authority. How you lay down rules, your brevity and firmness, your consistency and practicality: all of these qualities
are part of discipline. Once your child senses that you are
in control, you will find that punishment will be needed
far less, but if it is needed, you will make it stick.

Punishment is the clear, firm enforcement of a consequence for an unacceptable behavior that is within
the child's control and has been defined as relevant by
the parents. Ideally, the child should have been told
previously, in a calm discussion, what behaviors will no
longer be accepted. I believe that a punishment is most
effective when it is an objective, neutral act, and that
parents should try to be in control of their own emotions
when punishing. As you can see, this will require you to
start responding to your child's behavior in a different way.

Neutrality: Thinking, Not Feeling

Before you can deal with your child's behavior effectively, you have to adopt an objective attitude. The key
issue for you here is *neutrality*. Therefore whenever your
child misbehaves:

> • Don't respond emotionally or instinctively.
> Remember, your response must come from your think-
> ing, not your feelings.
> • Stand back and become as neutral as possible.

• Don't take it personally. Any time you say to
yourself, "Why is he doing this to me?" your feelings
are automatically involved and you are on the wrong
track.

• Focus on your child's behavior and not on his
motives or mood.

You are trying here to interfere with your custom-
ary gut responses to your child. Therefore, stop to think,
and hold back from your previous automatic responses
to his behavior: the immediate "no," the threats, the
feeling victimized. Try to disengage your feelings from
this process and replace them with the attitude of a
professor studying his subject. Aim for as cool an attitude of detachment as you can manage.

Does this mean that you have to become an automa-
ton of a parent who responds to his child only in calculated ways? Not at all! When you feel easier with your
child and more sure of your authority, spontaneity can
return. But you must remember that in a well-entrenched
vicious circle, the instinctive reactions are negative for
both the child and the parent. Furthermore, as I have
emphasized repeatedly, they are ineffective. The bottom
line in asking you to change *your* response is very simple: What you are doing isn't working! To learn a new
spontaneity, you have to pull back first.

If you can respond to one unpleasant situation out of
three in this way, you're on the road to success. Don't
get discouraged if it doesn't work every time. Unlearn-
ing old habits doesn't happen overnight.

Ask Yourself: Is It Temperament?

Any time you can relate a behavior to a temperamental
issue, you will be in a much better position to know
what to do about it. If a behavior stems from temperament, the child in a sense "can't help himself." Try to
recognize these situations. If you can see this linkage of
the difficult temperament to the trying behavior, your
attitude will automatically become more sympathetic.

During your five-day study period, you have focused on behavior, temperament, and the link between the two. Continue to practice looking for this link and to add any new observations. (In Chapter 8 you will learn techniques for managing temperamentally related behavior.)

For now, whenever your child does something annoying or irritating, ask yourself whether the behavior could relate to temperament. Your child has a temper tantrum. What set it off? A new piece of clothing? A crowded department store? Don't overlook the smallest factors. Does your daughter tantrum when you ask her to change her underwear? Ask yourself what the new underwear is like. Is it purple instead of white? Your child may be extremely sensitive to color as part of her low sensory threshold. And she will express that sensitivity vigorously.

You should also be looking for transitional situations, because they can precipitate problem behavior in children with poor adaptability. Simply calling your child in from lunch when he's been playing outside may provoke a stormy protest. So when your child gets upset, step back and try to see if there is a change involved: a breaking away from routine, a shift in activities, an alteration of pace can make the child resistant.

Ask Yourself: Is It Relevant?

As you have already seen, over-punishing is ineffective and simply acts to perpetuate the vicious circle. You want to punish much less, but much more effectively.

As you identify the "can't help it" (clearly temperamentally related) behavior and, eventually, learn to deal with this differently—through management rather than punishment—you are more or less down to the "Relevant Behavior" list you compiled in the previous chapter. This kind of more "naughty," often manipulative, behavior *can* be helped by the child; and if he has been clearly told that it isn't allowed, he needs to learn that there is a consequence if he deliberately misbehaves.

Punishment Is Symbolic

In my experience, the extent and severity of a punishment is not nearly as important as the *attitude* with which you punish. Five minutes alone in his room makes nearly as big an impression on the child as sixty minutes. In fact, it's not reasonable to expect a small child to stay in his room for a long time.

You're not losing your authority if the punishment seems "light." The fact that you're outlining what you'll do and then following through makes it effective. So as a general rule, make the punishment reasonable, and remember to punish with a serious, even menacing attitude. "Menacing" does not mean acting frightening, but only that your tone should convey that you are in control and very serious. Let your child know that you mean business. He won't know this if you simply continue to do what you have always done. Some parents have found it helpful to practice a serious facial expression and firm tone of voice in front of a mirror. Once your child starts to realize that you *really* mean it when you threaten, you will often find that all it takes is the simple "menacing" statement, "You'll be in trouble with me if you don't cut that out at once!"

Be Clear About Rules and Consequences

Any child functions best when he knows that his parents mean what they say. A specific misbehavior that is not permitted in the home should always be followed by a specific consequence. Your rules should be clear-cut and easy to comprehend. In this way your child knows exactly what's expected of him. It's a *rule*.

You have already decided on some basic rules and explained them to your child as simply and objectively as possible: "There is a new rule in the house. From now on, you are not allowed to hit anyone. If you ever do that, you are going to be punished by being sent to your room." And the first time your child tries to hit his sister, it's okay to remind him. But when he does it again, you act speedily and effectively. And you follow

through with your punishment. He hits, he's told he
broke the rule, he's sent at once to his room.

Punishment should be administered as quickly as
possible following the behavior. Don't delay.

Punish Only for Behavior

If your child behaves in a way that you have made clear
to him is unacceptable, he certainly should be punished.
However, you don't want him to feel worthless just because he misbehaved. Try to avoid terms like "bad boy"
or "bad girl." You want to convey that you disapprove of
a specific behavior, not that you don't like your child.

It is in this context also that you should avoid looking for motives. This can be hard to do, but there is a
reason for this suggestion. Of course all children, including difficult ones, have motives for some of their actions.
The problem in the case of a really difficult child, however, is that the behavior is often so hard to understand
that parents *assign* motives that may have nothing to do
with the child. Therefore, especially in the early stages
of applying the program, you will do best to suspend this
process of looking for motives.

Finally, don't confuse "bad mood" with bad behavior. I know that a whiny, sulky child can drive parents
crazy, but try your best to stay focused only on his
behavior, not his mood.

How to Punish

Be brief: Always be very brief with your explanations when you punish your child. "You've done this, it's
not allowed, your punishment is this." Never say more
than that. Don't overexplain.

For example, you have a pretty polished wooden
desk in your living room. Your son likes to put his toys
on it and play there, and you're concerned that he might
scratch it. A parent who really wants to explain everything might have said:

"Johnny, this is a very valuable piece of furniture. If
you put your toys on it, especially your toy cars and

trucks, there's a pretty good chance you'll scratch it.
And if it gets scratched, Mommy has to get the furniture
store to come and repair it, which costs a lot of money.
And Daddy will get really mad. So don't play on the
desk."

Instead, you should be offering one warning and one
warning only:

"Johnny, you know you're not allowed to play on the
desk, and if you do, I won't let you watch the cartoon
special tonight." If Johnny defies you, you now say, "OK,
that's it! No special tonight."

Don't negotiate: The problem for many parents of difficult children is that the child has become so powerful
in their eyes that they feel they're dealing with another
adult, so that they have to explain all their actions and
decisions. But with difficult children, you don't negotiate; you lay down rules. And if your child asks you why
and it's a behavior you consider relevant, answer, "Because I say so" or "Because that's the rule." This is not
to say that you should become an arbitrary tyrant. In
fact, your new rules will probably make a good deal of
sense to your child. The aim here is to assert your
authority in an objective and neutral way.

For example, let's say your daughter spits out food
at mealtimes and you have decided this behavior is
relevant. You tell her in advance, *away* from the dinner
table, that she'll be sent to her room if she spits out food.
She does it once and you give her the first and only
reminder that she'll be punished by being sent to her
room. She does it again.

You do *not* engage in the following dialogue:

"All right, Jennifer, go to your room."

"Mommy, please, I didn't mean it that time, it was
an accident."

"Well, I really meant what I said."

"Oh, but Mommy, you gave me this icky meat loaf
and it's so hard to eat, it got stuck in my teeth."

"You're supposed to go to your room now."

"Please, Mommy, please, I won't do it anymore, really, this is the last time."

"Jennifer—"

"Maybe I could just go to the living room instead?"

This scene should be replaced with something like the following:

"All right, Jennifer, you were warned, you did it again, now you have to go to your room for five minutes."

"Mommy, please, I didn't mean it that time."

"Go to your room. No more discussion."

"Why?"

"Because *I* say so!"

The ideal "political structure" for the family of a difficult child is modeled after a benevolent dictatorship rather than a democracy. The child gets *no vote* in deciding what his punishment should be. Remember again: You don't want to become a tyrant, but you do want to be an effective leader.

Be firm: Instead of yelling or screaming at your child, practice a more ominous tone of voice. Sound like you *mean* it. With a young child especially, tone of voice is very important.

Do not sweet-talk your child as if you don't really intend to act on what you're saying:

"Now, honey, we don't like it when you draw with your crayons on the wallpaper. Good children don't really do things like this, okay? All right, sweetheart? Next time you make a pretty picture, do it on a nice piece of paper and give it to Mommy."

Instead, be firm:

"I don't want to see you *ever* drawing on this wallpaper, or anywhere else except in your coloring book. Do you understand?"

Many parents don't realize how often they ask their young child to approve of their actions. A mother who says, "Now go to your room—OK?" is effectively undermining her own authority. Does she expect her daughter to say sweetly, "Yes, Mommy, it's perfectly all right with me to go to my room"?

Be aware also of how you use personal pronouns. "It's time for *us* to go to bed," carries a different message from, "It's *your* bedtime now!"

Don't warn too much: There are two aspects to excessive warning. The first is that your child may test you to make sure you mean what you say. When this is the case, it is important to carry through on what you've told him and not give him repeated warnings with no follow-through. One reminder is fine, but after that, *act*. A firm tone of voice and manner must be employed.

You do not repeatedly warn:

"Susan, don't play with Mommy's expensive new watch."

"Susan, if you play with Mommy's watch you'll be punished."

"Susan, what did I tell you about playing with Mommy's watch? Now, this is the last time I'm going to warn you."

"Susan! Did you hear me? I said *not* to play with this. Once more and you'll be in big trouble."

Instead, one warning and then *action:*

"Susan, if you play with my watch again you won't get a lollipop after lunch."

"That's it! No lollipop." (And, at a practical level, remove the watch.)

Parents often don't follow through with their threats. But if you keep your punishment simple and brief, and the child knows what he's not allowed to do, things should become simpler and clearer.

There's another kind of warning, which can be "too much"—warning in anticipation of your child doing something wrong. This can happen when your child has someplace special to go (e.g., to his grandmother's house). A mother might do the following throughout the hours that precede the visit because of her fear that something will go wrong:

"When you go to Grandma's, make sure you don't touch anything in her room. She gets very upset when you do."

"Now remember, at Grandma's you're not going to touch anything, okay?"

"I don't want to see you touching Grandma's things, right?"

Do your warning when you arrive at Grandma's:

"Remember that you must not touch Grandma's special things, they might break. If you do, you won't get any nice cookies and milk."

Be practical: Punishment depends on its context; be flexible about what you can do in any given situation. You have to free-lance sometimes and be inventive with what you can do with your child. And remember, too, that the age of the child must be taken into account. You might not want to send a 2-year-old to his room if he doesn't understand and won't stay there. But that child will understand if you take away an episode of *Sesame Street* or a snack he likes.

You might have to improvise. A child misbehaving in a shopping mall cannot be sent to his room then, and you don't want to delay your action until you get home. You might tell him that he won't get an ice cream cone if he misbehaves.

Be single-minded: Remember that the goal of effective discipline is to get your child to obey you. His attitude when he does this is not important. He may need to save face. Don't confuse this with disobedience; the message of the punishment still gets through. For example, when your child disobeys and you tell him he is being punished and must go to his room, he might say, "I don't care, I didn't want to be here anyway," and run off to his room. Ignore this and consider the punishment still valid.

Methods of Punishment

As you can see from everything I have said in this chapter, punishment is only one part of a more general attitude of adult authority. Once the other aspects of an effective disciplinary system are in place you don't need twenty-five different methods of punishment. You probably need only two or three, such as sending the child to his room for a short time or withdrawing a privilege. Also, remember once again the importance of tone of voice and a serious, firm attitude, especially when dealing with a younger child.

Many parents ask about physical punishment. I believe there is nothing wrong with a parent deliberately, and in control of their own emotions, occasionally using a smack on the rear. This can clear the air and bring the incident to an end very quickly. However, hitting a child when you have lost your temper is a very different thing indeed, and should be avoided. I also think it's wrong to humiliate a child by hitting him in the face.

If your actions are firm and brief, and part of an effective disciplinary system, they are not even really punitive. In fact, you are offering your child choices and following through with clear consequences. Say, for example, that even after establishing a bedtime routine and eliminating most of the ritual bedtime battles, your 4-year-old daughter continues to come out of her room repeatedly. Tell her, in a serious, calm discussion, that she has the choice of staying in her room with the door either open or closed, but there is no other option. When she comes out that night warn her once, but then, without discussing it further, simply march her back into her room, close the door, and hold it shut from the outside for two minutes (a long time for a small child). She is likely to get very upset. Grit your teeth, but hold firm. When you let her out, wait for her to calm down, and then say, "You see, Mommy and Daddy are serious about this. You still have the same choice. Now let's try again." You may need to repeat this sequence a few times, but if you do your part in a simple, relatively friendly, but very firm way, your chances of succeeding are greatly increased.

These principles of effective discipline are absolutely indispensable in your efforts to regain a true sense of adult authority with your difficult child. In fact, many parents have also found them very helpful in dealing with less difficult children. As you practice and refine your disciplinary methods try always to aim for an attitude which is kind, yet firm; absolute when dealing with truly relevant misbehavior, yet flexible with minor annoyances; friendly and very much on your child's side, yet very clear about who's in charge. You'll soon feel a much greater sense of control and your relationship with your child will improve. But this is only half the story, because in the next chapter you will learn some specific techniques for "can't help it" behavior that arises primarily from your child's difficult temperament.

8

MANAGING TEMPERAMENT
Understanding in Action

The principles of adult authority you learned in the previous chapter do not stand alone. In fact, they must be used together with a set of management techniques based on your new understanding of your child's temperament.

Management, as distinct from punishment, is used with a difficult child when the adult decides in effect that the child "can't help it." Mostly this occurs when the parent can make the linkage between the behavior and the underlying temperament. However, management also can be used for some types of wear-and-tear behavior, such as excess fearfulness. The parental attitude when managing is generally more sympathetic, as distinct from the tougher approach used when disciplining or punishing.

As with discipline, management may be generally divided into two categories: on-the-spot reactions, and the planned actions you devise at other times to prevent or minimize temperamentally difficult behavior.

LABELING: UNDERSTANDING YOUR CHILD

Now that you are a fledgling expert on many facets of your child's behavior and his underlying temperament, it is time for him to see that you understand him. The first step in this process is called *labeling,* and you must discard your everyday impression of what a label means. The term, as used here, refers to identifying the temper-

141

amental basis for a behavior, putting a name to it, and either sharing that information with the child or using it yourself to alter your attitude. Basically you are saying to your child, "I understand what's going on with you." Drop all ideas you have that the term "label" is pejorative or hurtful, because as used here it not only serves the function of increasing your and the child's understanding; it also reminds you of the neutral, objective, but kind and friendly stance you must take with your child.

Your attitude is one of the key issues here. You cannot apply a label or use any of the techniques, for that matter, unless you are neutral and sympathetic. Of course, this is difficult; emotions with these children run very high. You won't achieve instant neutrality, but *give it time*. The label will help remind you to be neutral. But sometimes you'll jump down your kid's throat, and sometimes you'll forget to label. Remember that there will be many more opportunities. You must build on the occasions on which you have success with the techniques, even though these may be few initially.

If you understand something about a child and share it with him, that child will gradually respond to the change in your attitude. As parents you are trying to set up communication with the child based on your true understanding of the important issues for him. Instead of reacting to what you think the child is doing to you, you try to make a firm but kind statement related to his temperament.

Here's an example:

Not: "You are driving me crazy."

But: "You are getting overexcited."

Another example:

Not: "Why do you always give me a hard time about going to bed?"

But: "I know that some nights you don't always feel sleepy at your regular bedtime."

By thinking of the label, you begin to think about the issue of temperament. And then you translate that information into understandable language. You would not say, "I know you have a low sensory threshold and therefore are sensitive to the feel of certain things," but rather, "You're very sensitive to the tags on clothes." Be specific, be neutral, and don't use any emotional words. Keep your label as cogent and as simple as possible.

Labeling, which is essentially an on-the-spot statement in response to a behavior, is one part of showing your child that you understand him. With children over the age of 3 years, simple, planned discussions about their reactions to change or sensitivity to clothes can also be very helpful. And once the child is able to recognize some of his temperamental features, he will gain more self-control. Well-managed difficult children can say to their parents, "I'm not used to it yet. Give me a little more time."

Here are some suggested labels. You may use these, or your own labels, provided you keep them simple and kind, and remain calm. Your tone of voice is important, because any words can sound highly charged when spoken emotionally.

TEMPERAMENTAL TRAIT	LABEL
High activity level	You're overexcited. You're too revved up. You're beginning to get wild.
Distractibility	I know it's hard for you to pay attention.
High intensity	I know you have a loud voice, but . . . I know you have trouble speaking softly, but . . .
Irregularity	I know you're not hungry/sleepy right now.
Negative persistence	I know it's hard for you to give up when you really want something. You're getting stuck.

TEMPERAMENTAL TRAIT	LABEL
Low sensory threshold	I know you feel hot when other people don't. I know this sweater doesn't feel right. I know certain things smell/taste/look funny.
Initial withdrawal	I understand this is new for you. I know it takes you time to get used to a new place. I know that new places (people, situations) give you trouble.
Poor adaptability	I know it's hard for you to make a change. I know you're really busy, but you are starting to get "locked in." (Teach the child what the term means.)
Negative mood	In the case of mood, the label is not for the child but rather for you. It helps you not to feel angry with a child who complains and criticizes in an unfamiliar situation, even one that would make other children happy. To yourself, you would say, "This is the way he is; he can't help it."

The technique of labeling is merely the foundation for a new approach to your child's difficult temperament. What follows is a description of specific management techniques designed to both prevent and cut short the most common problem behaviors resulting from that difficult temperament.

WILD BEHAVIOR

Wild behavior is most often seen in *highly active* children who are very excitable and get into an escalating sequence. The child starts off active, gets excited, gets overexcited, gets wild, and then loses control. The golden principle is **early intervention**. You need to spot the danger signs, get neutral and label, then intervene.

The key issue for the parent or teacher of a highly active, excitable, impulsive child is to learn to identify the point when the child is getting overexcited, then step in and act accordingly. You want to get to the child *before* he is wild and out of control.

Often this is a very subtle shift and not easy to pick up. You should observe your child in a wide variety of situations in which his behavior goes too far, to see if you can spot the progression. Decide for yourself at what point the child goes from third gear into fourth and then into overdrive. As a general rule, you can tell yourself, "Fourth and overdrive are *out*." You don't want to act so quickly that you intervene when he gets somewhat excited. That's a little too soon. You don't want to be on top of your child constantly. However, you want to avoid the dizzying escalation that occurs if his behavior goes unchecked.

At times, some children escalate very rapidly to the point where they lose control. In these situations you will be too late to prevent the outburst. Highly impulsive children may occasionally push, grab, or strike out with no warning. It is very important to remind yourself that this kind of wild or impulsive behavior is, for the most part, *not* in your child's control, and should not be punished. There is a difference between deliberate misbehavior and impulsive loss of control.

Once you start looking for this point of change in behavior, you will learn to defuse most situations before they go too far. The goal of your intervention is to get the child out of the situation. If you catch the escalation early, you may be able to simply **distract** him to do something else. At other times he may need to **cool off** or to **blow off steam**.

Cooling off is a technique used when the child is about to get wild. You get neutral, go up to the child, make eye contact, label "You are getting too excited," then tell him it's time to cool off, and if necessary, physically remove him. Or, if you become expert at spotting the early changes in his behavior, you might be able to give him a warning, "You're going to get too excited. Calm down or you will have to stop what you're doing."

You should designate some special "cooling-off activity" that calms the child down:

• For a young child, it might be a special book or record that you share together.
• With a small child, it could be as simple as, "Come and sit on my lap."
• Most highly active children love water play. Put them at the sink or in the bath and let them splash a bit. (This works well not only when the child needs to cool off but also when you need a half hour to yourself.)
• A favorite television program can work, and if you have a video recorder, you might tape a favorite TV show so you can replay it when necessary.
• If your child enjoys a special snack treat, such as ice cream or a piece of fruit, you might make the giving of the treat and the sitting down and enjoying it into a cooling-off activity.

Whatever the cooling-off activity is, it should introduce the fact that the child is now going to switch gears and try to calm down. Be clever and resourceful, and don't think of these cool-offs as rewards for bad behavior.

When a child has gone too far by the time you intervene, simply remove him from the situation entirely, deal with the tantrum, and let him settle down rather than allowing the escalation to proceed. In this case, you don't even want to talk to him. Just pick him up and get him out of there. If you have the space in your home, try to designate a room or part of a room as a special "cooling-off place." Keep this area simple. Remember that enforcing a cooling off is not a punishment but a sympathetic technique for dealing with overactivity that goes too far. Try to stay kind and friendly.

You may also have to go the opposite way, which brings us to the second form of intervention, **blowing off steam.** A very active kid can go stir crazy in a city apartment or stuck in a house on a rainy day. You can see them escalating there as well, though the buildup may not be a matter of minutes but may take place over half an hour's time. Here, too, you label: "I know you're feeling antsy."

Then choose an activity that allows the child to vent some of the energy. Go to the park. If it's raining, take him to the basement of your house and let him run. Turn on some music and dance. Be friendly: "Hey, I know you're getting crazy from too much sitting. Let's move around!"

In fact, if you use these terms—"cooling off" and "blowing off steam"—around your child, he'll get used to them and will come to know what they mean.

Always remember that the earlier you can get to the escalating behavior, the easier it is to intervene. But a hovering, "on top of my kid" parent can get too involved and end up watching the child like a hawk, ready to jump in at the slightest sign of trouble. You should try to keep a balance. And you will not have success each time.

If you miss the point of change to overdrive and the child gets wild, you'll probably lose your neutrality as well. Don't get discouraged. Just aim for objectivity the next time. Behavior doesn't change overnight, and there will be times when things end up wildly and with a temper tantrum. (Later in this chapter there will be a section on managing temper tantrums and other out-of-control behavior.)

RESTLESSNESS

With *active, distractible* children, a **sense of timing** is very important, especially in school and with homework. A parent or teacher should ask herself, "How long can he stay with what he's doing?" You can see the child getting restless, fidgety, losing concentration. He may start to move around in his seat, stare into space, scratch his head, fiddle with his pencil and paper. This is behavior that can precede "revving up" and that indicates the energy level of the child is starting to build.

There is a technique called **time out** that you can use in this situation. Tell him, "I can see you're getting restless." Then let the child take a short break and assign him something that will release a bit of energy. A "time out" is often used as a punishment for misbehavior, as when a child is sent to his room or told to leave the classroom. As I use it, however, a time out is *not* a punishment, but rather another form of early intervention. In school, a teacher might ask the child to come up and erase the blackboard, go into the hall for a drink of water, carry a message to another teacher, or help perform a chore such as putting away books. At home, the parent might tell the child to carry out a small task such as emptying a wastebasket, emptying the dishwasher, or setting the table. You can let him play with his toys for a while, or use one of the suggestions for blowing off steam.

During activities such as homework or mealtimes, a parent who has acquired a sense of timing with her child can actually use a **planned time out.** If you can see that the child can only "hold on" for ten minutes before he starts to rev up, let him take a break every ten minutes— allow him to leave the table, walk around a bit, and then return. This approach is also very valuable to the teacher of a highly active, distractible child.

There are two other things to keep in mind with restless, excitable, impulsive children. Parents and teachers often point out that they may not be present when the child escalates into an out-of-control state. The explosion may occur in the lunchroom or in the playground. There is very little you can do about such after-the-fact situations. Long discussions aimed at finding out "what really happened" are both frustrating and pointless. Nor does it make any sense to punish the child for behavior you didn't witness and which the child probably couldn't help. Try to limit yourself to a brief statement such as, "Bad luck. You must have lost control. Try harder next time." And see if you can arrange for closer supervision of the child in unstructured situations.

(Sometimes children, whether temperamentally difficult or not, are *deliberately* unpleasant or aggressive. This kind of behavior is calculated rather than impulsive, and if witnessed by the adult, should be handled much more strictly. Here punishment is certainly appropriate.)

This brings me to the second point. These highly active children thrive on structure. Your child will generally do much better if you can introduce more routine, calm, and predictability into his everyday life, both at home and in school.

Now of course this degree of supervision is not always possible for a parent or a busy teacher. If a child is repeatedly aggressive the teacher will come under pressure from the parents of other children. It may be better, when everyone is up in arms, for you to keep your child home for a few days to allow the situation to settle, and the whole question of whether this is the class or school for him may need to be looked at carefully.

DEALING WITH CHANGE

Once again you are going to look for the temperamental issue underlying the surface behavior, be neutral, and label it. In the case of change, the issues are *poor adaptability* and/or *initial withdrawal*. The key techniques to understand here are **preparation** and allowing the child **time to get used to it** in a new situation. It is very important for you to differentiate between preparing your child for a change and overwarning him. Anxious mothers "prepare" a child for a new situation by repeating, over and over, their fears about the child's behavior: "We're going to a birthday party this afternoon, and I don't want you grabbing for the cake. You should behave yourself at birthday parties." Later that day, the mother might repeat, "Remember, at that birthday party you should behave yourself." Or the over-explaining mother might say, "Today we're going to visit your friend Claire. We have to leave the house and catch the bus. Remember the bus stop, where we usually wait? We're going to get on a number ten bus, that's the big blue bus you always see. Don't you recall when we went on it last week and you saw the woman with the twin babies? You talked to the babies and they laughed. . . ."

This kind of repetition or overexplanation results in the child picking up on the mother's anxiety. Instead, the mother should make a temperamental statement to the child about the upcoming change: "You are going to a birthday party this afternoon and I know it's new for you, so if you want to stay close to me until you're used to it, that's okay."

How do you tell the difference between preparing a child and warning him? If *you* are anxious and repeating yourself, you're probably warning. If you're briefly and neutrally focusing on approach/withdrawal and adaptability, not too far in advance, you're preparing.

Remember, too, that what may seem to be an ordinary situation for you, as an adult, might be new and difficult for a child. A mother who thinks, "My child doesn't have to be prepared to go to a birthday party because she's been to other parties" is forgetting that each party has new children, new food, a new environment, or new entertainment. To a child, each party is different. So you must be sensitive about what might affect your child.

Time to get used to it is just as valuable to you as to your child. Knowing that your child holds back in new or unfamiliar situations will allow you to feel more relaxed and not to pressure him. In turn, the child, knowing you are there as a support, will generally venture forth more readily. Maintain a balance, however. He can stay close to you, but he doesn't have to sit on your lap.

The principle of allowing these shy, poorly adaptable children to proceed at their own pace is also extremely important for teachers. Such a child may take weeks, even months, before he participates fully in the classroom. Don't confuse this with anxiety and don't think of it as an emotional problem. By all means gently encourage the child to join in, but don't pressure him, and try not to see his shyness as reflecting negatively on your ability as a teacher.

Poorly adaptable children usually will do better if they are briefly told about the **sequence of events** in a planned outing or trip.

For example: "We're going to your friend's today. First we'll leave the house, then walk to the bus, then ride on it for half an hour, then walk to John's house."

Or: "Let's go for lunch. We'll get in the car, then we'll drive to the supermarket to pick up some juice, then we'll go to McDonald's, then we'll come home in time for *Sesame Street*."

A key aid in helping poorly adaptable children get used to change is called the **changing clock.** This can be used with children 2½ years of age or older. It's a battery-operated digital clock (seconds are not necessary) with a set of numbers that show time in a readout: 6:45 or 11:15, for example. The clock should have no other uses in the house and should be specifically identified in the child's mind as a vehicle for helping him with changes. Personalize the clock, if you like, with colorful stickers or your child's name. Tell your child that the clock is going to help him change from one activity to another and help him finish what he's doing before he starts something else. For example, your child may have a problem leaving whatever activity he's involved in and going out with you in the car. You can tell him that with this clock he's not going to have as much trouble making that change. Then you begin to use the clock each time a significant change is to occur and use it for *nothing else*. (Remember that during the study period you have learned what changes give your child trouble.)

Here's how this technique can work. You have a wading pool in your backyard. Your daughter likes to play outside, splashing in the pool, pouring water on the ground, having a wonderful time. When you call to her to come into the house for lunch, she resists, and generally this ends in a fight or a tantrum. With the changing clock in hand, you now go outside to your child and show her that the clock says 12:10. "When the last number changes from a zero to a five, you must come into the house and have lunch."

Poorly adaptable children hate to be surprised, and this gives them a chance to prepare for a transition within a limited time frame set by something neutral (the clock) and not you. Use the clock for any significant changes—to signal the nearness of bedtime, time for school, shopping excursions, the end of TV watching—anything you wish to prepare the child for. But don't overdo it. Like any other technique, the changing clock will lose its effectiveness if you use it twenty times a day.

In time some older children learn to cooperate very well with techniques for dealing with change. They will ask how much longer they have or ask to stay close to the mother in new situations, or say they need a little more time, or even use the changing clock themselves. A more harmonious, cooperative attitude replaces stubbornness, resistance, or tantrums. Learning to deal with change is an important step in breaking the vicious circle.

UNPREDICTABILITY

Parents are bewildered by a child's erratic behavior, and lack of predictability is especially bothersome in two key areas: appetite and sleep. It is extremely difficult to deal with a child who isn't hungry and sleepy at about the same times each day. Parents and children involved in conflicts over sleep and meals usually end up caught in the vicious circle of escalating demands and excessive punishment; this is one of the most exhausting of areas. The temperamental issue is *irregularity,* and the key is to **separate bedtime from sleeptime, mealtime from eating time.**

Children who are not sleepy will fight tooth and nail over going to bed. This can become one of the most inflammatory of family issues. You, as a parent, have the absolute right to enforce a bedtime, but you don't have the right to force your child to fall asleep. Purchase a small night-light. When bedtime arrives, the child has

to get into bed. The light is switched on, and the other
room lights are turned off. The child is permitted to
have one or two small toys or books in bed, or to have a
record or tape playing softly. But he is not to get out of
bed. This is *bed*time. However, it is *not* sleeptime. He
will sleep when he is tired, which may be at a different
time each night. But he will be *in* bed at the same time
each night. Your chances of success will also be increased if you lead up to the bedtime with a structured
routine, as described in the previous chapter.

Allowing the child to have books or toys in bed
should be treated as a special privilege. You may tell the
child that if, now, he gets out of bed, he will no longer
have this privilege. But if you find that your child is
unable to stay in his room alone even with a night-light
and with toys in bed, you may be dealing with fearfulness rather than defiance. Later in this chapter you will
learn some techniques that will enable your child to
cope with his fears.

Following the same principle, you cannot force a
child who is not hungry to eat at your regular mealtime,
but you can insist that he sit at the table with the
family while they eat. He can have a glass of juice or
only part of his meal while you eat, and he can contribute to the family conversation and interaction.

Use your judgment as to how long you should expect
your child to sit at the table. Remember your sense of
timing here; a young child won't last as long as an older
one, and active children in particular will have trouble
sitting still for long.

If the child is hungry between meals, he should be
given something to eat. This is *eating time*. You need a
balance here. The mother shouldn't become a short-order
cook. Keep these non-mealtime snacks simple; a sand-
wich will do or a bowl of soup and some cut up raw
carrots. You do not have to put meat, potatoes, and two
vegetables in front of your child each time he eats. You
can also freeze dinner food, or simply refrigerate it, to
serve to your child later.

A valuable technique with irregular children is the
goody plate. Allow your child to select anything (within

reason) he wants that might fit onto a dinner-sized plate: carrots, cookies, raisins, cold meat, cheese, potato chips. Then tell the child if he is hungry between meals he may have anything he wants *from the goody plate*. This technique can also be used with children who call for milk or cookies or water endlessly from their beds at night. A goody plate can be prepared and left on the bedside table.

Always remember that while *mealtimes* are to be decided by you, the child's appetite can't be controlled.

Unpredictable children may be erratic in their moods, as well. This poses more of a problem, for basically there isn't anything you can do about it. Learn to ignore these mood changes. A few things will help, one of which is internal labeling, telling yourself, "This is my unpredictable child." Another is not taking these mood changes personally. In general, this kind of moodiness improves as the family tensions lessen.

NOT LISTENING

"He never listens to me," many parents say, implying that the child is wilful and defiant. In fact the temperamental issue is usually *distractibility*. These children have trouble concentrating when they are not interested. The wrong way to think about this is, "He's not listening on purpose, because he doesn't want to listen to me." Rather, you should think of your distractible child who has trouble paying attention.

The important technique here is to **establish eye contact**. Make eye contact with your child before you tell him what you want him to do. Make sure he's not "out to lunch." It is extremely important to handle this neutrally. By saying, "Look at me!" in an angry tone of voice, you are building the reverse of what you want. So get neutral, label (to yourself, "This is my distractible child and he's unable to pay attention"), and get the child's attention. Say, "I want you to look at me and listen to what I have to say." Remember also to **keep it short and simple.** The child will tune out if your instructions are complicated or long-winded.

This is a critical issue with teachers in school as well. Their most frequent complaint about distractible children is that they don't listen. You can suggest these techniques to your child's teacher, pointing out that the child should not be placed in the back of the room but rather toward the front, where the teacher can have frequent eye contact with him.

WHINING AND "UNHAPPY" BEHAVIOR

Parents with whiny children are caught up in the vicious circle because they are trying to *stop* this behavior without realizing what's beneath it. The temperamental issue underlying much of whiny, cranky, "unhappy" behavior is a *predominantly negative mood*. A positive-mood child may whine occasionally, but it won't go on as long as the whining of a negative-mood difficult child. These children often seem to be in a "bad mood." They tend to be solemn or serious. They don't express emotions enthusiastically and often seem "sulky" to their parents.

If your child expresses things more negatively than positively, you can assume that this is in part temperamental. And if you have a child who withdraws in new situations and has a negative mood, he won't simply withdraw, he'll withdraw and whine and criticize: "Why don't we go? Why do we have to be here? I don't like it here!" With a child who is persistent, the whining may go on a long time; he gets locked in, and he'll go on and on and on. Negative mood greatly intensifies other difficulties. Parents get quite upset with these children, feel guilty that they can do nothing to please them, and fit problems increase.

There is no "technique" for dealing with negative mood. Your key principle here is **realization,** shifting your point of view to recognize that this is temperament, that negative mood is the norm for your child. You can't do anything about it except to *label* the negative mood (to yourself, *not* to the child) and then to ignore as best you can the expressions of this mood.

Parents often think something is really "wrong" with these children, that they are unhappy or even depressed. But this is not so unless the unhappiness has started recently, in which case it is not an expression of temperament. Recognizing that your child's negative attitude is rooted in his temperament is not always easy, but this understanding will help you not to overreact; and again, as the family atmosphere improves so will the child's attitude.

"I DON'T LIKE IT" BEHAVIOR

This kind of behavior is most commonly associated with *low sensory threshold*. This involves your child's sensitivity to feel, taste, smell, sound, temperature, lights, or colors. Again, parents often find themselves trapped in a vicious circle, especially if their children are highly persistent in expressing their preferences.

In this area, **labeling** is extremely important, part of the recognition that the child is not simply being contrary but is definitely bothered. Don't challenge his threshold. Instead, recognize it with a label:

"I know you don't like loud music. . . ."

"I know it doesn't feel right when your sneakers are done too tightly. . . ."

"I know you don't like the taste of ketchup. . . ."

"I know you get hot very easily. . . ."

Sensitivity to the feel, texture, and color of clothing can be particularly vexing, especially for the fashion-conscious mother of a cute little girl who absolutely refuses her mother's demands that she "look pretty."

The principle here is **not to challenge threshold** but rather to treat behavior related to it as irrelevant. The child's "taste" and comfort are represented by threshold. What's the point of making an issue over it? There are surely more valid ways to exercise your authority.

> • Your child likes to wear a pair of soft, old corduroy pants every day. You buy your child new pants of polished cotton. She refuses to wear the pants. You insist. But is it worth it? Should your child dress to be comfortable, or to suit *your* taste?

• Your child likes plain white cotton underpants. Grandma buys her bright blue underpants.
She won't wear them. It seems silly to you, but
is it worth it? She doesn't *like* bright blue because
it does indeed "bother" her.

• When your child's sneaker laces are tied, he
complains over and over again that they don't "feel
right." You get into constant fights over how many
times to do them over. But you could avoid the issue
by purchasing sneakers with Velcro closings. And
you could help yourself by recognizing that the feel
of the sneakers is indeed a threshold issue.

• Your child believes that purple, pink, and green
are matching colors, or that her party shoes go well
with her jeans. You are battling her every morning
over what she wears to school. Isn't that pointless?
Try instead to feel proud of her "flair" and ignore
the stares of the other mothers.

Similar questions of the child's preference often arise
around food issues. A child with a low threshold to taste
or appearance of food will often be extremely picky in
what he chooses to eat. It's best not to challenge the
child unless true nutritional concerns are involved, so
check with your pediatrician before you make food a
battleground.

Ask yourself why your child is insisting on her preferences. Work with your relevant behaviors in mind.
Many of these issues, when examined more closely, can
be ascribed to temperament, and it's best for you to back
off. This is the way your child is. It's a legitimate expression of her individuality.

If your child can't make up her mind or involves you
in a lot of back-and-forth arguments, you may avoid
power struggles by **offering a simple choice.** Instead of
picking out clothes for the child to wear, ask, "Do you
want to wear the blue shirt or the red shirt?" Both
choices should be acceptable to you, while also allowing
your child to exercise some freedom of decision. Decisions that seem insignificant to a parent can be very
satisfying to a young child. Beware, however, of offering

open-ended choices, which can result either in a frustrated child locked into his indecision, or a choice unacceptable to you. "What do you want for breakfast?" asked in the hope of finding *something* to please your picky eater, is almost certain to result in dissatisfaction for both of you: your child is unlikely to choose the breakfast you secretly hope he will, and he may also reject his own choice as soon as he sees it on his plate. In general, you are safest offering only two options.

Keep this technique in mind even when dealing with simple balkiness you might otherwise be tempted to discipline. "Terrible twos" who refuse to hold their mother's hand crossing the street have been known to relent when offered a choice of "right hand or left hand." Or you can ask, "Will you hold my hand, or do I need to carry you across the street?"

Some children are easily overwhelmed in crowded, noisy, bright settings. They become *overstimulated* and may show this through "I don't like it" behavior. This also is a threshold issue and should be approached gently and sympathetically rather than by forcing the child.

"I don't like it" behavior may also be related to *initial withdrawal* or *poor adaptability,* especially in a *predominantly negative mood* child. The immediate rejecting or clinging reaction of such a child when faced with a *new* situation, food, toy, article of clothing, or stranger is due to his initial withdrawal and becomes another statement of "I don't like it." The technique here is to **introduce new things gradually,** with plenty of time for him to get used to them.

Take the case of the child for whom a parent buys a new toy, a large tractor-trailer truck. The child loves trucks and in fact has amassed a nice collection of them, yet when the new toy is presented to him, he does not seem to want it. In fact, he does not seem to like it at all. This is puzzling, since he already has similar toys. In this instance, you must recognize that even if the child does want it, to him it *is* something new, and this is what you might say: "I know you don't like new things, so we're going to give you plenty of time to get used to it."

With a child who responds badly to new clothes, you might give her a new dress, then hang it in the closet for a day or two. Then take it out and let her look at it for another couple of days. Following this, you could suggest that she try it on. This kind of recognition of her temperament will work much better than forcing the issue by criticizing her. You don't want your child to start believing that she is bad just because of the way she is.

The gentle, preparing approach can work for new situations as well, such as on the first day of school, when you might say to your child, "You are starting in a new class with a new teacher and there will be some children you know and some children you don't know. It might be hard for you the first day or two, but don't feel bad, it's okay, and Mommy will stay nearby for a little while until you get used to it."

To sum up, with anything new—clothes, toys, people, situations—the child needs time if he has trouble approaching or adapting, and your job is to provide that time for him without feeling that it's a direct challenge to you that he won't proceed at the other children's pace.

TEMPER TANTRUMS

What is a temper tantrum? As defined here, the term is not limited to totally out-of-control behavior, the sort of scene during which the child hits his head against the wall or breaks furniture. The definition is broader: It is any situation in which the child has an outburst of anger, crying, or screaming. It might be better, in fact, if you call these "temper outbursts" rather than tantrums so you aren't applying this section simply to extreme temper tantrums but rather to a wider variety of angry responses.

First and most importantly, temper tantrums can be divided into two types:

- the manipulative tantrum or outburst
- the temperamental tantrum or outburst

The fundamental difference between the two is this: With the manipulative tantrum, the child is trying to get his own way through the behavior. He might say, for example, "Give me a lollipop." The mother replies, "No, dinner is in ten minutes. You can't have one." The child starts whining, screaming, and performing to get the lollipop. When the child is doing this to get his own way, there is a conscious manipulative element involved. In other words, he is being naughty, and acting spoilt.

With the temperamental tantrum, the child's temperament has been violated, and thus he throws a tantrum. An example of this would be a *poorly adaptable* child who is asked abruptly to stop what he is doing and switch to something else, or a *highly active* child whose escalating behavior is getting out of control. In other words, "He can't help it."

How do you tell them apart? First, by recognizing the manipulation involved in one and the temperamental issue involved in the other. Also, the temperamental tantrum tends to be more *intense*. The child really gets out of control. The manipulative tantrum, because of its nature, implies lesser intensity and more of a conscious, planned quality. But they can, at times, look the same, and it is wise to remember that the distinction can be a bit artificial, since one form can lead into the other. A manipulative tantrum can slide into a temperamental one when the child gets locked into the tantruming; a temperamental tantrum acquires a manipulative quality when the child comes to understand the value of what he's doing.

Here are some guidelines to enable you to tell the two apart:

• The manipulative tantrum is less intense.

• The manipulative tantrum is clearly a result of the child's not getting something he wants. You don't have to look for the motive; it's right there.

• The temperamental tantrum relates to an underlying temperamental issue.

• If you look at your reaction neutrally, you will find that you feel sorrier for your child when he's having a temperamental tantrum. You may say to yourself, "He can't help it." With a manipulative

tantrum you may feel, "He's trying to get his way
with me."

Now that you are aware of the distinction between
types of tantrums, what do you do about them? Here is
where the distinction becomes useful, for you must approach them differently.

The Manipulative Tantrum

• Don't give in unless your original denial is
unreasonable. If you've decided it is unreasonable,
you're allowed to change your mind. But in all other
instances, you must send a message to the child that
tantrums don't work. If you give in repeatedly, you're
telling your kid that the way to get his own way is
by being a pest. Parents who give in to such tantrums will soon find that their whole attitude to the
child becomes tentative and indecisive. The primary
issue in any dispute becomes to avoid the tantrum.
This is a real example of the tail wagging the dog.
Instead, tell your child, in a planned quiet discussion, that he will *never* get his way through tantrums and start to enforce this new rule.

• Your attitude toward the child should be more
menacing; be tougher and more firm. Don't be too
sympathetic. Do not say, "I'm sorry you're upset and
crying, perhaps you can have a lollipop later" but
rather, "You cannot have this lollipop, that's all there
is to it, and I want you to control your behavior."

• Distraction is a valid technique. It means doing
something practical on the spot to get his mind off
what's causing the tantrum. It is not the same thing
as giving in.

• Sending the child away is appropriate. You
could say, "You have to go to your own room until
you calm down." Even better is to remove yourself
from the situation.

• Ignoring the behavior is the best approach to
aim for if you can't remove yourself. Try to act

disinterested and, most important, don't negotiate the issue.

• Of course, if your child begins to hurt himself during a tantrum—for example, by banging his head on the floor—you should intervene. If you send him to his room and he continues to tantrum there with the door closed, go just inside or watch from the doorway to see that he does not hurt himself. Do the minimum you have to in order to ensure his physical safety, but otherwise keep your attitude distant.

It's easier to deal with a manipulative tantrum if you have a consistent approach all the time. Lay down the ground rules in a planned discussion, and then be firm, don't give in, be authoritarian, ignore the outburst, bring it to an end, don't get involved in discussions, be a little menacing, or send him to his room. Do any of these things, in any combination, but do them consistently. There will be examples of how to do this in specific situations in the next chapter.

The Temperamental Tantrum

• These tantrums are more intense, and there is more of a feeling that the child is out of control. When you realize that "he cannot help it," your attitude should be kinder and more sympathetic.

• With these tantrums you should be physically present with your child, with your arms around him if he'll permit it or just there with him as a comforting physical presence in the room. Be calm and say reassuring things: "I know you're upset, but it will be okay." If he wants to be alone once he calms down, respect his wish.

• There should be no long discussions of what's bothering the child, unless *he* wants to talk about it, and even then only once the tantrum is over.

• Distraction may be used if you can.

• You may simply have to wait it out if your child is highly intense [loud] and the tantrum is long. Have a pair of earplugs and some aspirin available for yourself.

• If you can recognize the challenge to her temperament as the reason for the tantrum, correct the situation if you can. For example, you put a wool sweater on your child, and she tantrums to protest against the way it feels. If you allow her to take the sweater off, the tantrum may not end immediately, for the child might be locked in, but the tantrum will not go on as long as it would have if you had not allowed her to take the sweater off. This is not giving in; rather, you, as an enlightened parent, understand the real reason for the tantrum and are attempting to correct it.

Again, you want consistency but, as distinct from the manipulative outburst, you are more sympathetic, reassuring rather than menacing; you stay with the child and you change your mind more readily.

With both tantrums it is extremely important that when the outburst begins, you stand back and look for five to ten seconds to figure out what's going on. What kind of tantrum is occurring? Your approach depends on this determination. Once you have decided, you will take one of two tacks:

• *You are menacing and firm.* "There's no way you're gonna get this, kid," when it's a manipulative tantrum.
• *You are kind, sympathetic.* "I know this is tough for you, I'll help you to bring it to an end," with a temperamental tantrum.

With either tantrum, when it occurs in a public place, *get the child out.* You'll achieve nothing by embarrassing the child or yourself. There's no point trying to stick it out, especially if you recognize a temperamental tantrum and you don't want people criticizing you for being so "nice" to your child during a tantrum.

LOCKED-IN BEHAVIOR

The *highly persistent* child who won't give in, the *poorly adaptable* child who doesn't tolerate change, the *low threshold* child with strong preferences, can get locked into a ritual with the parent that may escalate into a full-fledged struggle. For example, the child says, "Mommy, tie my shoes." "Okay," says Mommy, and she ties them. "Mommy, they don't feel right. Tie them again." "Okay." "Mommy, they feel *horrible,* tie them again!" The technique here is simply to **bring it to an end.** Every time the child asks and the parent does it again, you are pushing the situation into a higher level of difficulty. A child can start out with a threshold issue (such as shoes not feeling right) and then become locked into the "do it again" cycle. And once this happens, the more you try to please the child, the more the sneakers or hair barrettes don't feel right, the more she complains, and the more *both* of you get locked in and upset. This kind of interaction also fosters the doormat mentality in mothers who go to any extreme to please their child. The cycle has to be brought to an end.

But how do you recognize what's going on, and what do you do?

Essentially you must recognize that after a certain point you are no longer providing relief. Realizing this, you could say to your child *before* you begin to tie his shoes, "I know it's hard for you to get just the right feel of your sneaker laces. But if I tie them over and over, you will get more and more upset. So from now on, I will retie your sneakers twice, and if they still don't feel right, you'll wear something else." If it is essential that the child wear sneakers (for gym class, for example), you could end by saying, "Then it's too bad, but you'll have to wear them."

The critical issue for parents locked into power struggles with stubborn, difficult children is to recognize that repeatedly going back and forth on *any* issue is not only ineffective, but also actually *perpetuates* the struggle. I immediately know the parent is on the wrong track if there is a lot of argument, negotiation, or explanation involved. In such a situation not only the child *but also the parent* is getting locked in.

But *how* do you bring it to an end?

The answer is: **focus on process not content.** This sounds complicated, so let me clarify. The important thing for you to realize is that *the child is stuck.* What he or she is stuck on is *totally unimportant*! It doesn't matter whether she is repeatedly asking for a lollipop, or TV, or to stay up late, or whatever. What matters is the process of being stuck; and the more you explain or negotiate the more locked in the child (and you) will become. Recognize this early, stand back, get neutral, and say very firmly, "You have asked for ——— three times already. You are not going to get it. You can ask two more times and then you must stop!" "But what if she doesn't?" parents ask. Half the time she will stop, because you have directly addressed the issue of her negative persistence. The other times, simply tell her that there is nothing more to discuss and ignore her. Go to your own bedroom if you have to and close the door. And later, at a quiet time, explain to her that you understand that when she really wants something it's very hard for her to give it up, but that from now on whenever Mommy says "no," she really means it, and the child will have to accept this.

In these instances neutrality, firmness, and labeling are extremely helpful to you, as is this maxim: Remember that it will never get easier the farther it goes along. So **take a stand early**. Going on with things only makes them worse.

This principle can be applied in a variety of situations with children who get locked in. I know I have advised you to be more accepting of your child's negative mood. This does not mean, however, that you have to put up with endless unpleasant expressions of this mood. For example, if your child goes on and on whining and complaining about something, it's perfectly all right to acknowledge his feelings (so that he knows he's been heard), but then firmly to tell him that you've heard enough and that it's time to stop complaining.

A lot of parents persist in these endless routines

because of the temper tantrums that result when they don't. You can't be sure that your child won't tantrum after retying number three versus number ten, but if your child tantrums after number three, you can be sure that he would have had a tantrum after number ten anyway. In the meantime, you have eliminated ten minutes of the vicious circle and reasserted, kindly but firmly, your position as the leader. By stepping away and recognizing the underlying temperamental origin of the problem, you will make it considerably easier on yourself and your child.

SELF-HELP TECHNIQUES

Until now, virtually everything you have learned has been focused on educating you, the parents, and other significant adults such as teachers, to deal with the difficult child in a more positive and constructive fashion.

But what about the child himself? Can anything be done to teach *him* better ways of coping with and controlling his own behavior and feelings? To a large extent this is dependent on the child's age, intelligence, and his level of maturity. Here are some possible techniques for the older child.

The Child as Expert

From the age of five onward—even four in some cases— your child can be gradually educated by you about her own temperament. This obviously needs to be done in calm, planned discussions. Make sure you get across to her that she is an individual, and that some of her behavior is an expression of this individuality, not a sign of anything "wrong" with her. You can help her to see, for example, that she is very enthusiastic but that this sometimes leads her to get overexcited. Characteristics such as persistence, withdrawal (shyness), low sensory threshold (strong preferences), irregularity, or intensity (a loud voice) can all be explained in a simple and friendly manner. Indicate to her that you are proud of the fact that she is her own person with her own feelings, reactions, and opinions.

Then tell her that sometimes the way she is can cause her to react a little too strongly, and that you want to help her learn some ways to control herself better. For example, you can teach her to identify, and to label for herself when she is getting too "antsy" so that she can ask you or her teacher for a time out; when she starts to get too excited or upset she can take a few deep breaths and count slowly to ten; when she gets too focused or stuck on wanting something she can repeat to herself what she wants three times and then try to think of something else; or when she is feeling nervous in a new situation she should wait a while until she feels more comfortable.

When children I have known achieve this kind of self-regulation, their sense of mastery—their pride in the accomplishment—is wonderful to behold.

The Child as Mentor

If your child has a problem with one particular aspect of behavior, you can help her get over that roadblock by putting her in the position of a teacher. By doing this you create in the child an awareness that she's in control, a sense of mastery. You can, for example, buy your child a doll, and if she has trouble getting used to new situations, ask her to teach the doll to get used to new situations. You might also get the doll a little changing clock and ask your child to use it for the doll. The child as mentor works very well with biting. If you tell her the doll has trouble with biting, and your child is the mommy and should be nice to her and teach her not to bite, you may get good results. A child who has trouble going to the supermarket or to a birthday party should be allowed to take the doll there and show the doll how to get used to going to these places. This technique can also be used to help her with certain fears. By teaching the doll to be braver, the child may conquer her own fear.

"The Brave Companion"

Difficult children's fearfulness may manifest itself strongly at bedtime. They can become intertwined with their parents and refuse to sleep in their own beds, or insist their mothers remain in the room with them. A child with this problem will complain of being afraid, of being thirsty, hungry, in need of a special story or song, and so on. This can be handled by giving the child a fierce stuffed animal and telling him, "This is your brave bear (or brave dragon or brave lion). He's going to help you not to feel so scared at night when Mommy's not there." The toy should be new and specific, just for this purpose. This may help to relieve the sleep fears.

These management techniques are offered as strategic *guidelines,* not as a complete catalog of responses. By being clever and resourceful, you will be able to contribute a great deal to the success of your program.

Remember also that your key to the application of all these techniques is a *sympathetic manner.* Your attitude is very important. You can never remind yourself too often that the whole theme of this section (and book) is temperament, temperament, temperament. Always look for temperament, and if you find it, manage it—with understanding.

9

PUTTING IT ALL TOGETHER
The Expert Response

How do parents respond in a consistent, effective way to the various and complex situations that arise every day in a family with a difficult child? In this chapter you will learn how to integrate what you already know about discipline (from Chapter 7) and management techniques (from Chapter 8) into a practical new way of dealing with your child.

This new way of responding is based on true adult leadership. It can be broken down into a series of steps. What you are about to read will seem like a great deal of information to process before you take action. You will think: "But if my child is starting to tantrum, how can I go through such a complicated procedure before making him stop?"

Don't be discouraged by the apparent complexity. Don't expect yourself to "get it" immediately. With repeated practice and increasing confidence in your parental authority, the whole sequence will eventually take you only a few seconds. It will become second nature to you. Without thinking, you will automatically slip into the right response. But it takes time! If you can gradually change your reactions over several weeks, you are doing just fine.

The sequence of steps in the expert response to any difficult, negative, or "obnoxious" behavior goes like this:

1. *Can I deal with it now?* You want a quick take on yourself, on your state of mind. If you can't deal with it,

disengage as quickly as possible. If you can deal with it, move on to Step 2.

2. *Become the leader.* Stand back, get your feelings out of it, become neutral, and start to think.

3. *"Frame" the behavior.* Recognize the type of behavior from your behavioral profile.

4. *Is it temperament?* Try to link the behavior to the child's difficult temperament as defined by his temperamental profile. If it's temperament, the response in such a case is management rather than punishment.

5. *Is it relevant?* If the trying behavior is *not* based on temperament, is the issue important enough to take a stand on? If not, let it go, or respond minimally and disengage.

6. *Effective punishment.* If it's not temperament but it is relevant, respond firmly and effectively.

Let us now look at the expert response in greater detail.

Step 1: Can I Deal with It Now?

Your child is misbehaving, causing you problems, having a tantrum, whatever. Your first step before responding will be to take stock, to become aware of where *you* are. You will ask yourself, "What's my general feeling for my situation today? Am I all right with myself, my husband, my kids?" You want to focus on yourself in a *general* way. Are you upset because you had a fight with your husband last night? Is it simply a "bad day" for you?

If you are aware that you are tense, upset, nervous, or feeling ill-equipped to face anything, then this is not the time for you to attempt anything heroic. The less you do, the better. Your main goal is to disengage. Get out of the situation and/or get the child out of the situation.

Let's see how this would work. You have a rotten headache, and your once-every-other-week housecleaner just quit. You need to run an errand, but your child is very involved with a puzzle, and it's raining outside. She protests loudly when you try to prepare her for the trip. This is not the time to risk a major blow-up. Postpone your trip and take care of your headache. If your child has spilled your cosmetics, you might just simply take him out of your room, sit him in front of the television, and close your bedroom door so he can't get back in.

If, however, your state of mind is relatively okay, your answer becomes, "Yes, I can deal with it."

Remember always: If you can't deal with it, disengage.

Step 2: Become the Leader

This is a critical step because it involves the objectivity so essential in dealing with difficult behavior. Your leadership posture starts with standing back and consciously making your attitude neutral. The key is not to respond emotionally or instinctively:

Get your feelings out of it!
Try not to act like a victim!
Think and evaluate!

Say things to yourself such as: "What's going on here?" "I am the adult." "I am bigger, stronger, and smarter." "I am the boss." "I am the expert on my child."

Remember always: Be neutral—don't respond emotionally.

Step 3: "Frame" the Behavior

The objective here is simply recognition. You are looking for a pattern and trying to put the child's behavior into a category. Focus always on the behavior; try not to think about the child's motives. Groupings of behaviors and the settings in which they occur are listed in Chapter 6. Ask yourself questions such as, "Have I seen this before?" The idea is not to be surprised, confused, or thrown by anything your child does.

Remember always: Look at behavior, not motives.

Step 4: Is It Temperament?

Another way to pose this question is, "Can he help it?" Here you are trying to relate the behavior to an underlying temperamental issue. By now you should be fairly expert on this. (If you need to, refresh your memory by glancing at the temperamental profile in Chapter 6.)

Any time you can link the behavior to temperament, quickly change your attitude to one of sympathy and understanding, and proceed to manage the child rather than punish him. Do this by making eye contact, labeling, and applying a technique. You may still be firm, but your attitude is one of helping your child through a rough patch.

Remember always: If it's temperament, manage.

Step 5: Is It Relevant?

What if you can't relate the behavior to temperament? You've decided he *can* help it. But do you punish him or not? It depends on how important the issue is. As parents you have already negotiated a final list of relevant behaviors—those behaviors both of you will always take a stand on. Therefore you should be able to decide quickly whether the behavior is relevant or not. If it's irrelevant, your objective is either to ignore the situation entirely or to respond minimally and disengage. Your general attitude in dealing with irrelevant behavior is casual, light, and somewhat disinterested. Ask yourself questions such as, "Can I lose by doing nothing?" "Can I let this behavior go?" (For more details, review the "relevant behavior" list in Chapter 6.)

Remember always: If it's irrelevant, do as little as possible.

Step 6: Effective Punishment

This is your "big gun." Use it only for *relevant* behavior. By now your child should have been told about the new rules in the house. *He* knows what behavior will always be punished, although he doesn't use the word "relevant." Therefore, if he deliberately breaks a rule, he should be punished. If there is time, you can give him one warning, but *never more than one*. Refer to your three types of punishment: e.g., sending him to his room, withdrawing a privilege or possession, or a smack on the rear. Choose one punishment quickly and then apply it briefly and without overexplanation or negotiation. "You know you're not allowed to throw your plate on the floor. Go to your room for five minutes." If he refuses, take him by the hand and march him to his room. Your general attitude should be firm and somewhat menacing. You can *sound* angry, but try never to lose control yourself. A firm reprimand spoken menacingly may be all the punishment needed for a younger child. (For more details, review "Effective Reactions" in Chapter 7.)

Remember always: If it's relevant, punish briefly.

Some final words of advice. Be practical. Use your common sense and imagination. For example, if your child tantrums in a public place get him out of the situation quickly and take him to a quieter area. Sit in the back seat of your car, for example, if there's no place else to go. Retire to the bathroom. Your common sense and practicality as a parent can contribute enormously to the success of your effort. And at times (e.g., with dangerous behavior) this whole decision-making process goes out the window and you'll simply react to what your child is doing, as when he runs into the street or climbs too high in a tree. Go ahead and act. The idea is not to suppress your common sense and all your natural instincts.

That's all very well, you may be saying to yourself, but how does this system work in real life? Here, to illustrate, are ten family vignettes based on the experiences of parents in my practice. Each captures a typical situation in the day-to-day life of a difficult child. Each is followed by a suggested **reaction,** an immediate response to the child's behavior, and a longer-term **planned action** designed to address broader issues.

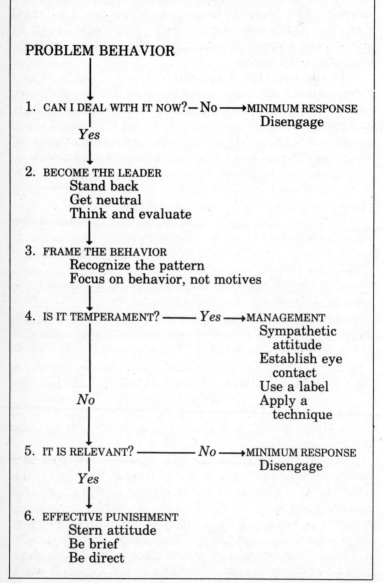

THE EXPERT RESPONSE
A Decision Tree for Parents

PROBLEM BEHAVIOR

1. CAN I DEAL WITH IT NOW? — No ⟶ MINIMUM RESPONSE
   Yes   Disengage

2. BECOME THE LEADER
   Stand back
   Get neutral
   Think and evaluate

3. FRAME THE BEHAVIOR
   Recognize the pattern
   Focus on behavior, not motives

4. IS IT TEMPERAMENT? —— Yes ⟶ MANAGEMENT
                                        Sympathetic
                                          attitude
                                        Establish eye
                                          contact
                                        Use a label
   No   Apply a
                                          technique

5. IT IS RELEVANT? ——— No ⟶ MINIMUM RESPONSE
   Yes   Disengage

6. EFFECTIVE PUNISHMENT
   Stern attitude
   Be brief
   Be direct

As you know, planned actions refer to the various methods of discipline or management that can be used to improve the child's behavior and the general family atmosphere. Planned actions are carefully thought out and discussed *in advance, away from the heat of the moment.* The child is in a way a "partner" in these methods. They are used to help with issues such as transitions, sleep problems, or to offer inducements for changing behavior.

In addition they include the clear definition of new rules, expectations, and consequences, setting up morning and evening routines with or without a star system, and introducing the changing clock or other methods of preparation, the brave companion, the child as mentor, and instituting rewards for specific behavior. The details may be found in Chapters 7 and 8. You will see here how useful they can be in preventing the recurrence of problem situations.

Remember always how important it is in these discussions to define the issues first between the parents, to be clear and specific with the child, and to ask him kindly but firmly to try his best.

One note of caution: Please don't regard the following suggestions as "recipes" for your family. Your own successful solutions will be based on your study of the entire program and on your growing understanding of your child's unique temperament.

"WHY CAN'T YOU EVER LIKE ANYTHING?"

The Gordon family is on a family excursion. The parents have bought tickets to *Sesame Street Live* in the city and are taking the children to see it. Their older child is a well-behaved, outgoing 6-year-old. The younger child, Deborah, is a serious, shy, sometimes clingy child. Her parents have spent a lot of money in hopes of pleasing her. She is 4 and has rarely enjoyed any children's movies or shows. But she adores "Sesame Street," especially Big Bird. They bring her to the theater where the show is to be performed, but she whines and clings and won't

go in. Then she is afraid to sit in her own seat and
insists on sitting on her mother's lap. When they finally
quiet her, the show begins and the live characters appear. Big Bird arrives and Deborah whimpers with fear.
The other children are all laughing with delight and
calling out, "Big Bird, Big Bird!" But Deborah can't be
consoled. Her mother is furious. "What's the matter with
you?" she angrily whispers to her clinging child. Deborah can't talk but finally chokes out, "I'm scared." "But
that's Big Bird, your favorite from TV." "No, he's not,"
Deborah whines. "He's not the same." The parents are
forced to take their crying child from the show and
return home, angry and convinced they have failed again.
Their child, they fear, will never like anything.

What would an expert parent do?

Reaction: The Gordons could have behaved differently with Deborah both when she was first clingy, and
later when she was frightened at the sight of Big Bird.
By becoming neutral they are able to stand back and
frame their child's behavior. Where had they seen this
before? Deborah is being shy, particular, and complaining in a public place. Is temperament involved? Clearly.
This is Deborah's response to newness, her initial withdrawal. She is also easily overstimulated and is somewhat overwhelmed in the theater. Her poor adaptability
makes her very aware that Big Bird is "not the same."
Her seriousness and complaining reflect her negative
mood.

If her mother and father realize it's temperamental
and that Deborah needs reassurance, her mother will-
ingly takes Deborah onto her lap, gets close to her, and
says quietly, "I know this is all new for you and you're
not used to seeing Big Bird this way, but it's okay, and
you can take your time getting used to him." She can
encourage the frightened child to take quick peeks at
the character. Then, if this fails and the child is still
upset, she can be sympathetically removed to the back of
the auditorium, where she might be willing to watch
from farther away.

Planned action: With a child like this, you can begin preparation the day before. Tell her the family is doing something new and you know she may need time to get used to things. Explain that she is to see her favorite characters for *real,* that they'll be the same but they'll look different, more colorful and much bigger. The day of the show, leave extra time so that when you get there you can stand outside and get used to the new place. This is a child who should be taken in early before all the seats are filled, shown her seat, shown the stage, shown the orchestra pit. If candy is bought for the family and the child refuses, save some for her for later when she's more used to everything. And the parents should discuss their game plan ahead of time. Decide who will sit next to her, hold her, and if needed, remove her to the back of the theater. Try not to dwell on how expensive your day is, how much trouble you have gone to, and how much you want her to like it. Remember, her predominant mood is serious, and don't expect her to show excitement or great pleasure the way her older sister does.

NOBODY WINS, EVERYBODY LOSES

Alice Blake has a hungry 6-month-old baby and a cranky 6-year-old difficult child who is entering the second week of first grade and not adjusting too easily. At 5:00 P.M. Alice realizes she is out of formula and has to take a quick drive to a local shop to buy more. Her husband can't be asked to fetch it because he is working late, so she walks into her daughter's room and interrupts her while she's playing with her dolls. "Please come with me a minute and go to the store. I need milk for your brother." The child refuses. She continues to play with her toys. Her mother tries to persuade her. The little girl says "no" again, more loudly. "All right," the mother says, "you can stay here and play with your dolls. I'll just be gone a few minutes. I'll lock the door. You've been by yourself before. It will be all right." "No!" the girl shrieks. "Don't go!" "Then come with me in the car." "No, no, no!" The child is screaming. The baby is also shrieking, with hunger, and the mother is desperate. "Look what you're doing to me. Look how upset I am. And what about your brother? He's just a little baby and he has no formula and it's all your fault!" The child watches as her mother storms out of her room. Then the child dissolves into a screaming fit and starts to throw her dolls around her room.

What would an expert parent do?

Reaction: The mother gets neutral, then frames the girl's behavior. This is her resistive, stubborn behavior, and the temperamental issue is that the child is not adaptable, and the change (from playing with her dolls to going out) is too quick. The mother has also, in effect, asked the child to decide whether to come along or stay in the house alone when the child isn't prepared to do either one. Also involved is the fragility of a child not accustomed to her new first-grade class and that of a child at 5:00 P.M., normally the "witching hour" for any kid. Realizing that this wasn't the time to leave the child alone, the mother should have said, "I know you need time to finish playing and I'm sorry we don't have much time today, but you can take your dolls into the car." If this does not help and the child is simply stuck and cannot choose to come or not, don't assume that she is frustrating you on purpose. It might be best to decide the formula can wait, feed the baby apple juice, and help the older, difficult child get over her upset. Be sympathetic and supportive if your child gets this way, but stay in charge and make the decision for her.

Planned action: This is a persistent, poorly adaptable child who generally needs to be prepared for transitions. The changing clock can be used. Tell your child, "In five minutes we are going out to the store. In ten minutes you will be back in your room playing with your dolls." Keep the context of your child's behavior in mind as well. When it is the first few weeks of school and your child is more fragile, don't try anything too sudden or unusual with her.

WHOSE BED IS IT, ANYWAY?

For a combination of reasons, Jason has been coming
into his parents' bed for a long time. But now, at 3 years,
6 months, he will not sleep anywhere else. The problem
began in infancy with frequent waking during the night.
When Jason began climbing out of his crib, he came into
his parents' room and climbed into their bed. Often they
were too tired to take him back into his own room, and
they let him stay. After a while he wouldn't go to sleep
in his bed, and his mother, worn out from this nightly
struggle, began putting him to sleep in her bed, then
transferring him into his bed later in the evening. The
evenings and nights have become a ritualized game of
musical beds, which is complicated by a recent onset
of fearfulness. Jason complains of fear of the dark and of
bad dreams. But each night, after a brief attempt to get
him to stay in his room, his mother gives in. His mother
and father have begun to have serious arguments about
how to handle the situation. The father has tried to
enforce a regular sleeptime for the boy and to make him
stay in his room. The mother, more protective, feels
sorry for the child and then relents, allowing him to go
to sleep in the parents' bed. The father is spending most
nights on the couch downstairs. "Whose bed is this,
anyway?" he protests to his wife.

What would an expert parent do?

Reaction: Not applicable. This problem can't be dealt
with on a night-by-night basis.

Planned action: The answer to a problem like this
lies in understanding it. Ask yourself some questions
about yourselves and your child. How much of this is
habitual, with the child and parents involved in a com-
pletely predictable nightly ritual? Is he coming into your
bed because he is afraid? Or has it also become manipulative? Are you confusing bedtime with sleeptime? (It's
true that habit, fearfulness, manipulation, and irregularity can become so intertwined that it is difficult to
tell them apart. You will probably have to try several

strategies to find the right combination.) An irregular child cannot be forced to go to sleep, but a regular *bed*time can be established and enforced. A child's fearfulness can be helped with a "brave companion": give the child a "brave bear" or some other stuffed animal that will protect the child at night. A doll can also be used with the "child as mentor" technique in which the child is asked to watch over the doll, as a "mommy" or a "daddy" would. If the child has a problem with nighttime awakenings and comes into your bed, then reassure him but try always to put him back in his room. Do this in a brief, firm manner. If he is scared, stay with him until he settles down, but don't get into bed with him. Be comforting, but don't do anything to stimulate him.

An evening routine is essential. It can be augmented with a star system. The routine should start well before bedtime with after-dinner playtime, TV watching, and bathroom activities in regular order preceding a soothing bed routine such as familiar stories; calming songs; and a good, secure round of cuddling—followed by bedtime (not necessarily sleeptime). A child may be allowed toys in the bed and a dim night-light; he is allowed to play for a while but may not get out of bed.

The specifics for dealing with bedtime problems may be found in Chapters 7 and 8. The main thing to remember is that you, the parents, have to be in charge. You may be better off, initially, just eliminating the nightly struggles even if it feels as if you are "giving in." Achieve some success in other, less highly charged, areas first. Then when you feel you have regained some of your adult authority, attack the bedtime issue in a coherent, planned, and consistent fashion.

THE PICKY EATER

Johnny's mother likes to cook and likes to feed her family good, nutritious meals. She reads cooking magazines for new ideas and believes firmly in balancing the family's diet. She invests a lot of time in planning and preparing the food. But her son, Johnny, now 4 years old, has been difficult to feed. He is rarely hungry at

mealtimes and doesn't like changes in his diet. Much of
what he eats tastes "funny." His mother is constantly
frustrated and feels rejected because he won't eat her
food and angry because she's spent so much time preparing it. She's also worried about his getting "proper nutrition." As a result, she is forever forcing, persuading, and
cajoling Johnny. Her son, on the other hand, pulls on his
mother throughout the day asking for something to eat.
Apples, bologna, cheese, crackers, cookies—he nags and
nags at her. She's always going to the kitchen to fix
something new. But when she gets the cheese cubed or
the apple peeled, he's changed his mind and doesn't
want any or takes only a small bite. Both mother and
child are locked into an endless, exhausting struggle
over food.

What would an expert parent do?

Reaction: Not applicable. The need here is to pull
back and develop a planned action.

Planned action: Johnny's problem is clearly related
to temperament. His irregular rhythms prevent him from
being hungry at predictable times. Because he is poorly
adaptable, he doesn't like changes in foods or the way
they're prepared, and his low threshold to taste adds to
the sensation that the food isn't quite right and tastes
"funny." But Johnny's mother should also do a bit of
self-evaluation. Is she simply concerned about Johnny's
being healthy, or is she also upset that he won't eat *her*
food? True concern for health might be served by taking
a child to a pediatrician. Let the doctor decide on the
child's nutritional state. When mealtime comes in the
home, Johnny should be required to sit at the family
table even if he is "not hungry." *Eating time* can be
whenever he *is* hungry. And if what the child eats is so
difficult an issue, or when he eats it, the mother can
prepare a "goody plate."

In general, if you have a picky eater, you should be
far more casual about diet. This may sound like nutritional heresy to you, particularly if you are concerned,
as some parents are today, that your child's irregular
eating habits may actually be contributing to his behav-

ioral problems. Let me put this concern into perspective. With a difficult child food may become a part of the vicious circle. A very stubborn child can become so caught up in a power struggle over food that he even refuses to eat a food he does enjoy. Therefore, your primary job is to get food out of the vicious circle. Check first with your pediatrician if you like, but try to disengage every time you feel your anxiety or your anger rising about food. By all means insist on *politeness*. Johnny should say "please" when he wants you to fix something special, and he should behave at the dinner table even if he is not eating. You can also set some limits. If he wants only hamburgers for lunch and dinner don't make an issue of it, but you can certainly say "no" (briefly and without negotiating) to candy just before dinnertime.

Your first goal with eating, as with sleep, is to eliminate all the emotionality and upset attached to what are fundamentally biological functions. Once you accomplish this and your family life is going more smoothly, you can return to questions of nutrition—with much more positive results.

ON THE ROAD

Jane Wilson does a lot of riding in her car. She lives in the suburbs, and to get to the supermarket or shopping malls, she has to drive on an interstate highway. The trips aren't very long, but traffic usually is fairly heavy and moves rapidly. She always feels she must pay close attention to her driving, particularly when she takes her two children with her in the car. The older, 6 years old, is a fairly well-behaved little boy, but her younger child is a 4-year-old terror, an extremely active, stubborn, impulsive child. It's often impossible to get this little boy strapped safely into his car seat. He sits in the back behind the driver, next to his brother. On this day, he is louder and squirmier than usual, having been interrupted playing on the swings in the backyard. He yowls his protest loudly from his place in the car's backseat. His mother, trying to concentrate on her driving, shouts back, "Be quiet!" The little boy is getting revved up and wild. He picks up one of his sand toys, kept in the back of the car for beach trips, and begins to hit his brother with it. Toys start flying. The next thing the mother knows, she is hit in the head with a metal sand pail.

What would an expert parent do?

Reaction: The first thing to do in a car when danger and safety are the issues is to stop the car. Pull over to the side of the road; on an interstate highway pull into a rest area or, if necessary, onto the shoulder of the road. Get calm. Recognize that this is "wild behavior." Then try to see if temperament is involved. It clearly is. You have taken your very active child from a "free" activity. He is going to be upset at being interrupted and at being in a confined space. Everything escalates from there. The child becomes wild and loses control. Bring your child to the front seat, get eye contact, and gently calm him down. "I know you were upset leaving the swings. I did it too quickly, and then it was hard for you to be in the car. Calm down. Everything's all right." Then leave the child next to you for the duration of the ride.

Planned action: Clearly, preparation would have helped this mother. Using the changing clock back home at the swings would be in order. Sitting the child up front next to you would follow. Let the child choose a few safe toys for seat play, and leave the rest locked in the trunk. And it might be wise to keep a little emergency bag in the car, perhaps under one of the seats, with special provisions for longer trips. You can include the child's favorite snack, some small cans of juice, a cuddly toy, and a few new objects that might interest a bored and restless child (a set of keys, an interesting box, brightly colored stickers). When your child is overexcited, cool him off *before* you embark on a car trip. Try to break longer trips up into segments, so that you can take him out of the car to "blow off steam" a little. And in general it is better to have the child sit next to an adult in the car.

MR. TANTRUM

On a brisk, wintry day in New York, a mother stares out
the window. She feels trapped. Her child is getting stir
crazy from staying in the house all day, but because it is
cold and getting overcast outside, she isn't sure if a trip
to the park is worth all the effort it will take to get him
ready. But after several unsuccessful efforts to entertain
him, he is getting more and more difficult and has already had two tantrums. She is ready for the confronta-
tion. She goes into her 4-year-old son's room. "Do you
want to go to the park?" she says. "No, no, no, no!" he
cries. "You can run around," she continues, starting to
pick up some of the toys he's flung around the room.
"No, no!" he continues to scream, starting to have a
tantrum. His mother is fighting to stay calm, not knowing what he wants or understanding what this is all
about. She steels herself for what is to follow. "We're
going out," she announces at last and drags him to the
bed. Eventually, sitting with him and talking to him,
she calms him down a little. She gets his sneakers. After
putting them on, she ties the laces. "No, Mommy, that
feels bad," he complains, and she ties them again. "No,
Mommy, I hate them," he whines, and she does the laces
over. Again and again they go back and forth, her tying,
him objecting. Finally he's screaming again and she's
waiting, exhausted, for the next step. She persists because she knows if she doesn't get him out of the house
she is going to go crazy. He refuses to put on his winter
coat and has another outburst. His mother insists, forcing him to wear his coat. She drags him out of the
apartment and into the elevator. When they get to the
entrance to the playground he refuses to go any farther
and starts to scream. Other mothers stop and stare. His
own mother has had it. "You're not going to do *this* to
me again." She tries to drag him into the park. After
much protest, he finally gives in, and once inside, goes
off to play with the other children. His mother sinks
down, gratefully, onto a bench. A short while later, he
comes over to her and asks for his big truck. "It's back
home," she tells him. "Go ask the other boys if you can

use their truck." "But I want mine," he insists. "Go and
get it." He begins to tantrum once more. His mother is
furious and feels totally victimized.

What would an expert parent do?

Reaction: This child has two kinds of tantrums,
temperamental and manipulative. A temperamental tantrum (over the issue of how his shoelaces and coat feel)
gets mixed up with the tantrums over getting his own
way (wanting his truck) so that his mother treats them
all the same. Remember how to handle each one—the
temperamental with some understanding and involvement, the manipulative by not giving in and by trying to
ignore it. Either way, it's OK to be firm. A good thing
for a mother to stress to a child like this is, "When I say
no, I mean it." If he continues to tantrum in the park,
take him home. She should also have brought the retying of the shoelaces to an end much sooner. It doesn't get
any easier if you tie them over and over. At the entrance
to the park she should label the child's initial withdrawal and then allow some time for him to overcome
this.

Planned action: This mother and child are clearly
caught in the vicious circle. Assuming that she has
learned some new principles and techniques, the first
helpful thing this mother might have done is to plan the
afternoon. She should have made the decision to go to
the park earlier and prepared the child. Her actions
shouldn't stem from desperation; this will only lead her
to attributing motives. *Keep your own feelings out of it*.
Decide in a neutral way, should I take him to the park
or not? Yes or no. The changing clock would help him
switch activities. On the issue of sneakers, set a limit on
how many times you do them over, and let the child
know. If it's a recurring problem, switch shoes. Or buy
sneakers with Velcro closings. If it's cold out and your
child refuses to wear his coat, have him carry it with
him. If it's really cold out, he'll want to put it on. But if
he really doesn't feel the cold the way most people do (a
threshold issue), forcing him to wear it will cause a

temperamental problem. Once at a place you've chosen to go, even if it's familiar to you, your child may still resist and need reassurance. Remember that this is an initial withdrawal, tell him you understand, and encourage him to stay with you until he's used to it.

YOU DESERVE A BREAK TODAY

The Wilsons enjoy their 5-year-old child, even though she's much more active than many of their friends' children. She can be impulsive, loud, and sensitive to changes in her environment. But she's an outgoing, positive child. The fact that Stephanie has two older brothers has helped her parents. Their family style allows her to be more active than another family could tolerate. The only problem arises when they take her with them to places where she's confined, such as restaurants. That's why, instead of going to a sit-down place with waiters, they've chosen to eat at McDonald's. It's fast, convenient, and there's a nice play area for the children. When they arrive, Mr. Wilson goes inside to get the order while Mrs. Wilson watches Stephanie in the little playground. After a short while, Stephanie starts to get too excited and soon becomes wild. Another child tries to take away her new doll. She loses control and slugs the child. Her mother will not stand for this. "You're a bad, bad girl," she says to Stephanie. "You cannot play here anymore." She takes the child inside with her to sit down. Stephanie is all revved up and won't sit. The mother, angry now, tries to force her. The child knocks over her drink, throws her french fries on the floor, and spits out her food. Her parents are very angry. Their lunch is ruined, and they don't have the option of letting Stephanie wander out to the playground.

What would an expert parent do?

Reaction: When Mrs. Wilson saw Stephanie getting too excited in the playground, she should have intervened and let the child cool down a bit. She could take her to sit in the car, or into the ladies' room, someplace quiet away from the other children. Get neutral, go over to your child, remove her from the play, make eye contact, tell her, "You're too excited," and go to another place. Stephanie should never have been taken inside without such a cooling off. If she gets too restless in the restaurant, she can be allowed to get down from her chair and wander around a bit. A sense of timing is important with this child.

Planned action: By using the cooling-off period with your child on a general basis, you should be able to intervene much earlier in situations like this one. The parent who watches the child will know when to step in before it's too late. She develops a sense of timing. If you live in a city apartment with a highly active child, make sure she gets outside enough to blow off steam. Try not to take her to "adult" restaurants where her behavior will embarrass you. And arrange for after-school sports or dance programs, or a special gym program for toddlers.

"IT ISN'T FAIR"

Michael is 7; his sister is 4. He thinks he lives in the most unfair house in the world because his bratty little sister *always* gets her way. She never gets punished; she does things he's not allowed to do; and she's horrible to him and he's not allowed to hit back. She is loud and rough. She can't share but always wants his toys. And when she wants something, she can go on and on about it. Her mother thinks that a big brother ought to make allowances for a baby sister. She feels two ways about her little girl: She knows the child is hard and that she gives her brother a very tough time, but she's also very protective of her little girl, who is so young and seems so fragile. The father, who is not home very much, thinks his son should be a "little man" and thinks it's "sissy" for brothers to have to watch out for little sisters. He and his wife fight about this a lot. The boy's favorite toy is his metal train set, which runs on tracks and has a station, trainmen, freight cars, coal cars, and a red caboose. He is very protective of this set, especially because he has to give in to his little sister on just about

everything else: sharing food, games, toys, and television time. And he feels she always gets what *she* wants.
But the little girl is fixed on this train set, and she
especially covets the red caboose. She has made several
efforts to take it away from her brother. One day she
enters his room when she was supposed to be playing
alone in hers, coming on her brother playing with his
trains. "That's mine!" she cries, grabbing for the caboose. Her brother has had enough. "No!" he yells as she
picks it up. She loses control and throws the train car at
him. It strikes his forehead. He screams and smacks her
on top of her head, hard. Their mother walks in on the
two screaming kids, who both yell, "Mommy!" But since
the little girl is more upset, the mother sides with her.
"Now, you know you're not supposed to be in here!" she
says, not at all angrily. "He hit me," the girl says. "She
threw my train at me," her brother replies. But the little
girl is sobbing more loudly and seems genuinely hurt.
The mother reprimands her son. "You know you're not
supposed to hit her," she says sternly. The boy is out-
raged. "You always take her side. It's not fair. What
about me?" When their father gets home, the boy is
sulking and won't eat and there's a nice-sized lump on
his forehead. The little girl is happily watching her
favorite TV show. Seeing his son, he asks what happened, and when he hears his wife's version of it, all
about "my poor little girl" and how her brother won't
look after her, he explodes. "That little girl is not a piece
of glass. Look at the kid's forehead. Can't he have some
time for himself?" They argue about this over dinner,
but nothing is resolved. The boy feels it doesn't really
matter what his father says. Michael is home most of
the time with his mother.

What would an expert parent do?

Reaction: Coming upon a children's fight when you
were not present to see what happened, you should not
try to be a judge. Don't try to assign blame. Simply
separate the children. Later you can ask yourself if,
for your difficult child, this is a temperamental issue.
But first you have to deal with the behavior, and here

the answer is to be practical but not to take sides. Talk
to the older and calmer one first. "I know you like to
play with your train alone. Let me handle your sister
first." Give him a reassuring pat and turn your attention to the out-of-control one. This is not favoritism;
it is practicality. Since she is having a tantrum, it's
best just to calm her down and settle her with something
she likes, a favorite toy or television. Then turn your
attention to the older child. Don't try to establish
fault, and don't punish either one unless you witnessed
the whole incident from the beginning.

Planned action: Find the pattern that leads to the
flare-up between your children. This will help you find
an answer. In this case the younger, difficult child controls the home and her brother. She feels *entitled* to play
with her brother's train set and persists in trying to get
at it. She gets locked into wanting the caboose. A firm
stand should be taken. She is not allowed to play with
her brother's toys without permission, or to enter his
room when the door is closed.

Other solutions for problems between siblings include:

• For children who fight over TV programs, it's
often easier to buy an inexpensive second television
set.

• If trouble between your children escalates when
they play together, watch them interact and try to
figure out what situations usually cause problems
between them. Make an effort to be there at bad
times. If you hear fighting escalating, go in, but
remember: *Don't take sides*.

• Talk to your older sibling about temperament.
Explain that the difficult child cannot help some of
the things she does. Explain that this is why she
gets extra attention. Take the time to do this; it can
really help the sibling to understand and make allowances. In addition, if you feel you have somewhat neglected your easier child, take some steps to
correct this. Plan some special time or occasional
outings just with the easier child.

• See if the rules you have established are in line with the needs of your children, or whether the younger child actually "gets away with it." Here the older child needs uninterrupted playtime alone with *his* train. Make sure he gets it.

• In general, most parents need to take more of a stand with their difficult child and to let up on the older, easier sibling. Difficult children are deceptive; they're much stronger than you think, and they do not benefit from being treated like fragile porcelain china.

"I DON'T WANT TO GO TO SCHOOL!"

Peter, just 6 years old, is an active child but one who holds back and clings at times. He tends to worry and bite his nails. His relationship with his mother is warm but somewhat too involved. He has just spent eight weeks in a summer day camp. After a hesitant start he has enjoyed the experience immensely—much more than kindergarten, where he had had a rocky year. He's been more confident, and his mother, Jill, has had a relaxed and fulfilling summer of her own. Peter would come home from his eight hours of camp exhausted and worn down, eager to eat dinner and go to bed. But camp has ended, there are two weeks to get through until school starts again, and the picture has changed during this time. Peter gets bored and cranky from lack of activity. Also developing is clinging, fearful behavior very unlike the Peter his mother had grown accustomed to over the summer. He will scarcely go out into the backyard alone to play. His mother reacts with irritation and annoyance that reflect her own difficulty adjusting to this transition time (though she isn't really aware of it). All she knows is that she's constantly yelling at her child. "Why can't you play on your own? Why do you keep hanging around me and bothering me?" She feels he's like a little shadow, always dogging her tracks. She has a list of things he'll need for school and is trying to get the chores accomplished. But each activity, haircut, new shoes, new pants, is a major battle. Peter clings to her and refuses to enter stores, let the barber touch him, try on the shoes. He won't even play with his friend next door, who has always been his closest playmate. His mother starts to worry about what all this means. She had come to believe over the summer that Peter had gotten "better"; he was cooperating in camp and enjoying his summer. There were few complaints from counselors. Jill had even begun to think that school wouldn't be a big problem. Now she's begun to wonder if Peter isn't "troubled" and to worry about what will happen when he enters first grade. "How will he manage without me?" she thinks.

And, of course, the first week of school is impossible. Peter won't let her out of his sight. She has to stay with him in the classroom. When she tries to leave, he gets hysterical. By the second week it's even worse. He is reluctant to get up and get dressed. He complains of stomachaches. He almost has to be dragged to school. He won't get out of the car and clings to his mother's legs when she tries to get him to enter the classroom. She doesn't know what to do. Should she go? Should she stay? Should she give in and let him remain home an extra day? Peter is now afraid to go to sleep at night. He says he's afraid of robbers and complains of bad dreams. Finally the teacher won't let Jill stay in the classroom anymore. Peter has a tantrum. Jill looks at the teacher, who remains firm. She looks down at Peter and says, "Let go of my leg." But she doesn't sound like she really means it.

What would an expert parent do?

Reaction: The response to a child's reluctance to go to school is based on understanding whether temperament is involved. In Peter's case, is it temperamental? Some aspects are, having to do with initial withdrawal and poor adaptability, but here temperament is not the only issue. Peter is also a somewhat nervous child who has developed what is known as "separation anxiety." With this kind of school refusal, the critical principle is to remember that *the child belongs in school and you have to leave.* This is absolute. You must go. You can be

kind, but you must be firm. And there should be no
ambiguity about it. Say good-bye matter-of-factly and
leave. Don't discuss anything, don't explain. The clearer
you can be in your actions with such a child, the easier
it is for the child. The longer you stay involved with his
refusal, the harder the situation will be.

Planned action: Several aspects come into play here:

• Mothers should be aware of their attitudes
when their children are home during transition times
between school and camp or during school holidays.
You are going to feel more trapped. Most mothers
do.

• What has happened to Peter during his time
between camp and school is that a period of growth
over the summer has been followed by regression.
This is quite common with difficult children and
should be handled *not* by pushing for more independence but by giving the child a secure base. For
example, don't be anxious about getting your child
to return to the backyard by himself if he expresses
fear about going. Tell him not to worry: "I know you
got used to having a good time in camp and it's
different when you're home, but you'll have a good
time here, too." During these times of transition be
friendly and supportive, and don't judge his behavior. However, maintain some balance. You don't want
to become so protective and involved that you hover
over him all the time. The child may feel braver
with his father, and the two of them should be doing
more together at this time.

• Don't get involved in lengthy discussions about
the fears. By all means let your child express what's
bothering him if he can, but then don't question him
a lot about it. If you do, you will in a sense be giving
the unreal fears (monsters, robbers, etc.) legitimacy.
It's much better to reassure the child briefly. Say
something like "Your mommy and daddy love you,
and we won't let anything bad happen to you."

• Prepare the child for going to school by talking about it to make it familiar but not overpraising

it or discussing it endlessly. Visit the school and look around; perhaps stop into the classroom if possible. But do this in a relaxed and casual way. Don't oversell anything.

• If you think your child needs a morning routine to be able to get ready for school on time, institute one a week or so before school starts.

• When school begins for your 5- or 6-year-old and he has a lot of trouble leaving you, try to arrange for a transitional adult to meet the child outside the school and take him in. This might be a security guard, teacher's aide, or teacher. Don't stay with a child of this age (but if your child is 2 or 3 years old, then, of course, you may remain). Remember that reluctance to go to school is a common occurrence and is not particular to the difficult child. However, regressive behavior is more common in difficult children; they won't become a bit more clingy but rather will be quite extremely clingy. If you find that you and your child are getting too involved in the mornings, let the father play a bigger role. Both parents should try to be neutral and kind but absolutely insist that the child go to school.

THE CLASSROOM TERROR

Patty has enrolled her 4-year-old daughter Allison in a church nursery school. Allison is "like a boy," very tough, active, bossy, easily overstimulated, and doesn't like changes. The parents have learned that she does best with predictable routines. Within a month of the start of school, Patty is getting phone calls and notes from teachers about her daughter. Allison hits and bites other children, throws toys, doesn't share, won't pay attention or listen, and refuses to participate in many group games. At home, Allison was never quite this difficult. She played happily with her two active older brothers and liked her routines. Her mother is baffled by this information. As the weeks pass, Allison begins to show signs of having problems at home, becoming unruly and difficult. Finally the school informs Patty that Allison is "too disruptive" and can't come back until "she learns to behave."

What would an expert parent do?

Reaction: Don't do anything right away. You might keep your child out of school for a few days while you figure out what's going on. Tell your child in a general way what you are doing: "We'll keep you at home a bit and try to make everything better." Set up a conference with the school. And do not punish the child or question her too much about what is going on. This final point is most important. Too often, when a young child has problems in school, the parents finish up lecturing and punishing the child for behavior they haven't even observed. This achieves absolutely nothing, other than to make the child see herself as "bad."

Planned action: If your child has trouble with transitions and with changes in routines at home, then in a school context she may well have some problems. High activity level and distractibility are important issues as well. Set up a conference with the teacher or teachers before school starts. Don't antagonize teachers by suggesting they might not know how to handle your child. And certainly don't apologize for your child in advance. Rather, approach them in a constructive way, saying something like, "I'd like to share some information with you that is helpful to me at home with my child. My daughter has a lot of trouble changing activities, and I have to prepare her for changes and give her extra time. Having an extra few minutes can really help. My child can also get very stimulated by active play and gets wild quickly when she's with a group of kids. I have to watch her because if she switches to high gear, she can get very wild. What really helps me deal with this is getting her away for a bit to cool off. Also, I do have a problem getting her to listen to me, and it really helps if I get her to look at me before I tell her anything. She will pay more attention when she sits closer to you." Base your suggestions on your experience as a parent, your expertise on your child's temperament, rather than telling them what to do as a teacher; this will set the tone for good communication throughout the school year.

These vignettes illustrate how the principles of adult authority and the techniques of management go hand in hand with an education in temperament to enable you to handle your difficult child. Progress will occur gradually, interspersed with rougher periods for both the child and the parents. Be patient with yourselves; be loving with your child; learn to appreciate his good qualities and to enjoy him. In time, the vicious circle will be replaced by liking and respect between you and your child.

10

COPING WITH A DIFFICULT INFANT
The First Year

How could a small baby be so much trouble? the parents
of 5-month-old Gayle asked themselves daily. When she
was born, she set up a howl that shook the nursery.
They worried about her loud crying and didn't understand why she was so fussy, cranky, and "unhappy."
They tried everything they could to cheer her up: new
toys, colored mobiles, making funny faces, rocking her,
changing her, wrapping her in soft blankets. But everything they did seemed to make her cry harder. They
were convinced they had the unhappiest baby ever. Was it
all *their* fault? Was there something wrong with Gayle?

◆

At the age of 6 months, Jonathan was never still, much
more active than any other baby his parents had ever
seen. He was always squirming out of his mother's grasp.
He had already fallen once from the bed and once from
the changing table; his mother had merely bent to reach
a clean shirt on the shelf below, and he had plummeted
to the floor. Now she felt she had to watch him constantly,
and the signs that he would soon be crawling brought her
more anxiety than pleasure. Another problem arose when
she introduced solids; he fussed and spit out anything new.

◆

Near the end of their first year with Seth, his mother
and father took a pocket calculator and tried to add up

how many hours of sleep they'd had since the arrival of the baby. They wanted to prove conclusively that they had less sleep than anyone else. Seth never slept at regular times. One night he might sleep for ten hours in a row, and take two naps during the day. The next day he might drop the naps and sleep for only five hours at night, waking up every hour or two to scream and fuss. The third night he might not sleep at all, but the naps might be taken the next day. His appetite and bowel movements were also unpredictable. Without a recognizable pattern to build on, his mother had been unable to establish any regular feeding or sleeping schedule. He was a fussy, fretful, cranky baby as well. The doctor had diagnosed Seth as "colicky," but his prediction that the colic would disappear by 3 to 4 months proved untrue. Now Seth's mother ruefully admitted that she had the world's only colicky 12-month-old, a bargain she hadn't expected.

◆

Do you recognize your baby in any of these three descriptions? Gayle is intense with a negative mood and has a low threshold to stimuli, while Jonathan is highly active and withdraws from new foods. Seth, with his irregular rhythms, is driving his family crazy.

It has become increasingly apparent from recent research that babies are born different. The New York Longitudinal Study conclusively demonstrated that temperamental differences are evident from earliest infancy, and there has been considerable focus in recent research on vulnerable newborns. Dr. T. Berry Brazelton, among others, has identified a group of "small-for-gestational-age" neonates. These babies often are thin and long, and their skin peels easily. They are irritable, hypersensitive, cry a lot, and their parents often say they look worried. They are certainly hard to deal with.

New parents are especially vulnerable, and unsure of what to do with a temperamentally difficult baby, and even the pediatrician may not be able to provide all the answers. Much of the behavior must simply be understood and accepted or contained. With an older child, a difficult temperament and parental reactions often result in the vicious circle. With the infant, on the other hand, the temperamental expression is purer, and the parents are not yet involved in the vicious circle.

Another difference is that parental concerns with the difficult infant center initially on "What's wrong with the baby?" rather than on "What's wrong with *me*?" The mother may be exhausted and bewildered, but usually she is not yet too caught up in feelings of inadequacy or depression. The marriage may be strained, but 6 months of hard labor is not the same as 3 or 4 years of it.

IS THE BABY REALLY "DIFFICULT"?

It will probably be several months before parents can begin to sort out temperament from other possible interpretations of the baby's behavior.

  • "Colic" is a common diagnosis during the first 3 or 4 months. Colic itself is an ill-defined entity. The term is generally used to describe a baby who is periodically irritable and fussy, and who cries or screams for no apparent reason. Many explanations are offered for why otherwise healthy babies scream in obvious distress and cannot be comforted. Many parents believe that colic is caused by digestive problems and that the baby will "grow out of it." Some doctors agree and say that colic is self-limiting and should disappear by 3 months. Others say that the term "colicky" simply describes the baby's behavior, may be due to other causes, and can continue beyond 3 months. My own belief is that so-called colic is frequently based on a difficult temperament.
  • Difficult behavior in infants can mimic other infancy problems. If your child refuses a bottle, perhaps he is teething or coming down with a cold. Since the baby cannot tell you, you must eliminate other possible explanations before concluding that his behavior is an expression of temperament, such as irregularity or oversensitivity to taste.
  • Problem behavior in an infant may also have some relationship to allergies. If your baby seems

intolerant of some foods (especially milk); if his nose often seems congested and stuffy; if he has rashes, especially on the face and behind the ears; or if he has bouts of vomiting and diarrhea, the possibility of allergies should be discussed with your pediatrician. There may be an overlap between allergies and temperamental difficulty.

• Finally, if the baby is extremely irritable, develops no schedule at all, cries constantly, and *fails to make normal progress as measured by weight gain and developmental milestones*, then something may really be wrong. You may not be dealing with temperament at all, but rather with a more serious problem that needs proper professional attention.

A TEMPERAMENTAL PROFILE OF YOUR BABY

Parents of infants up to 12 months old may find it useful to draw up a temperamental profile. Suppose that your pediatrician has assured you that your baby is both normal and healthy. How can you identify difficult temperamental features in an infant?

The traits that occur most frequently during the first year are irregular rhythms, high activity level, negative mood, high intensity, and low sensory threshold. Initial withdrawal and poor adaptability are the next most common. Distractibility and persistence are not evident quite so early.

Here is how these features show up:

DIFFICULT TRAITS IN INFANCY

High Activity Level
May have kicked a lot *in utero*. Restless in the crib; kicks blankets off. Squirms a lot, making him hard to dress and change and bathe. Has to be watched carefully to prevent accidents.

High Intensity
Cries loudly; screams. Shrieks with delight.

Irregular
Unpredictable biological functions. Feeding and sleeping are hard to schedule; may wake a lot during the night. Bowel movements may be irregular. Seems to have no "inner clock."

Low Sensory Threshold
Easily overstimulated. Startles easily and may overreact to light, noise, being touched, or to the feel of clothing or the taste of foods. Very sensitive to a wet or dirty diaper.

Initial Withdrawal
Spits out new foods, solid or liquid. Protests when first exposed to a new experience like a bath, a new carriage, a new toy, a stranger.

Poor Adaptability
Doesn't like changes in routine or schedule; protests by fussing or crying or screaming. Even after the initial response, takes a long time to warm up to new situations or people.

Negative Mood
Generally fussy or cranky. Not a "happy baby." Whimpers, cries.

YOUR BABY

	VERY DIFFICULT	MODERATELY DIFFICULT	MILDLY DIFFICULT
Activity level	☐	☐	☐
Intensity	☐	☐	☐
Regularity	☐	☐	☐
Sensory threshold	☐	☐	☐
Approach/withdrawal	☐	☐	☐
Adaptability	☐	☐	☐
Mood	☐	☐	☐

MANAGING YOUR BABY

Simply understanding what is happening with your baby can alleviate a great deal of guilt and worry. But there are also a few management techniques that can help. Here are some practical guidelines trait by trait. You will need to rely on your own day-to-day observations in adapting them for your baby.

Irregularity: The Unpredictable Baby

Most babies have an inner clock that plugs in at about 6 to 8 weeks of age; irregular babies do not. Therefore, *you* have to be his clock. Try, as much as you can, to create routines for feeding and sleeping. Even if the baby won't go along with the schedule, you should persist gently for five to ten minutes on each occasion.

How do you set up such a schedule? First, you must be aware of the two extremes to avoid. If, on the one hand, you try the demand feeding/sleep approach, you are going to be so spun around by the irregularity of your child that you won't know if you're coming or going. If, on the other hand, you try to impose the kind of clockwork schedule favored by your grandparents' generation, you will increase both the baby's distress and your own.

Daytime: With this in mind, try to plan a schedule that comes as close as possible to *any* pattern detected in the infant. Chart your baby's sleep and feedings over a week to give yourself clues. There may be only the glimmer of a pattern, but it should be used. Let's say, for example, that your baby is always hungry when he wakes in the morning, even though the rest of his day is total chaos as far as feeding is concerned. This is a golden nugget of something predictable. You should pattern your schedule around this one signpost and work from there.

Or perhaps you decide your baby should have a "regular" nap each day, but he is waking at different times each morning. You might wake him every morning at 7:00 A.M. to get him started on some regular schedule, and then put him down to nap at 11:00 A.M. Devise your schedule and then try to stick to it. Of course, you should not ignore your baby if he is screaming in his crib. But refrain from going in too quickly to pick him up if he cries between feedings or at scheduled rest times. Give him a chance to settle by himself. Babies have much more ability to calm themselves than we realize.

Here's how this might work in practice. Let us assume you have decided that the right feeding schedule is 9:00 A.M., 12 noon, 4:00 P.M. and so on. On each occasion, you should persist gently in trying to feed him for five to ten minutes, even if he seems uninterested. (You will feel more confident about this if you confirm your schedule with your pediatrician beforehand.) At 9:00 A.M., your baby refuses to eat and puts up a fuss for ten minutes, so you do not persist after that. But at 10:30 A.M., he is screaming with obvious hunger. What do you do? Hold out for noon, or feed the baby? The answer is to feed the baby at 10:30, but to feed as little as possible, just a small "snack" to stretch him out to noon. Use your judgment as to the amount that will pacify him temporarily.

Nighttime: Solving sleep problems is a good deal harder than dealing with eating irregularities. Daytime naps may have to be curtailed if the baby is an irregular sleeper during the night. You want to try to make the baby more tired. Some pediatricians instruct new parents not to let the baby sleep more than three or four hours at a time during the day. This is practical advice for all babies, but more important with irregular babies than with others.

Here are some other suggestions for dealing with sleeping problems:

• Don't reinforce the baby's wakefulness when he gets up irregularly during the night. When you go into his room, enter the same way each time. Keep the lights dim. Check to make sure nothing is wrong, settle the baby as quietly and firmly in his crib as you can, and leave. In general, it is not a good idea with these babies to pick them up, walk around, bring them into your room, or talk and play with them. Your first priority should be to settle them down.

• Sometimes you have to be practical. If you're not able to settle the baby and you're faced with screaming that goes on and on, choose a way to soothe the baby. This might include feeding, picking up the baby, walking with him, rocking, and so on. Experiment with different methods to find out which works best. Then *stick with this method,* and if you must take the baby out of his crib to soothe him, always do the same thing for approximately the same amount of time.

• If your baby is "up all night" during the first year, then make a plan to cope with it. You and your husband might alternate staying up, you for a few nights, then him; or divide getting-up time during the night into two halves, during which one partner sleeps while the other is "on duty."

• *You* should always be in charge of a schedule with your irregular infant, rather than just responding to your infant's irregularity. Be regular and predictable and never let the infant's unpredictability be translated into a chaotic family response.

If you have tried these approaches and your baby still has not adapted to a schedule, if you would be grateful to have a sleep cycle that lasts even five hours rather than two, then ask your pediatrician about the advisability of a mild sedative for your baby. Medications such as Benadryl or Phenergan are commonly used for sleep problems. But this type of medication can also be useful during the day for irregular difficult babies with no inner clock. Given in smaller, divided doses several times during the day, it may act as a calming agent and smooth out your baby's behavior enough to allow you to establish patterns—at which point the medication can be discontinued.

High Intensity: The Loud Baby

You cannot do a thing about this inborn propensity for your baby to cry very loudly. Some suggestions (and here you must be very practical) include: padding the

walls of the baby's room by hanging baby quilts and
blankets on them; putting down wall-to-wall carpeting
to absorb some noise; buying a "white noise" machine
for your own bedroom; and getting earplugs. Don't worry,
you'll still hear your baby cry—you just won't hear him
so loudly.

Negative Mood: The "Unhappy" Baby

Other parents' babies smile, coo, and gurgle. Yours
doesn't. In fact he is generally fussy. Although you cannot change your infant's basic mood, you can use the
technique of labeling to yourself, "This is the way he is.
It doesn't necessarily mean that he is unhappy." If your
pediatrician says nothing is wrong, realize that his mood
is not a sign of any real problem but simply a reflection
of your baby's makeup. His crying will lessen as he
develops other means of expressing himself.

Low Threshold: The "Sensitive" Baby

If you have a baby with a low sensory threshold, you
may have a baby who cries when you turn on his musical mobile over the crib, who startles at the sound of a
door slamming, who "doesn't like" being held, who pulls
away when you lean over abruptly and make funny
noises. This is a "jumpy" baby. The way to handle this
infant is to *reduce the stimulation* in his environment:
Don't use a lot of bright colors and patterns in his room,
don't hang busily moving mobiles over the crib, don't
put lots of toys inside the crib, don't let bright lights
shine in his direction. All these things, which might
delight another infant, will overstimulate the sensitive
baby. If you live in a noisy urban environment, you
might buy a "white noise" machine for the baby's room.
You can also carpet and pad his room to protect him
from excess noise. If outside light troubles him when he
naps, purchase blackout shades for the windows. Rocking often does not calm these babies because they don't
like being held and find the rocking motion too stimulating. Create a very soothing environment in which everything is simplified.

Some further suggestions for an easily stimulated infant:

- Don't play with your baby just before bedtime. Do soothing, calming things instead; if a bath calms him, move his bathtime up to the last activity before he goes to sleep.
- Work out by trial and error what settles him down (e.g., crooning to him, a radio playing softly, a small music box), and then establish a consistent routine using these cues both at bedtime and at naptime.
- Select toys carefully; certain toys may be too stimulating for your child. Find playthings with soothing colors, soft sounds, and smooth textures.

Low-threshold babies can be sensitive to the feel of clothing as well; if your baby seems unhappy when you dress him, consider allowing him to spend much of his first year dressed in just a diaper and a T-shirt. Infant nightgowns with the bottom drawstrings removed are also good, as are clothes made of natural fibers such as 100 percent cotton, which are softer to the touch than synthetics.

If your baby is highly sensitive to taste, "what baby likes" will have to be determined carefully. Different formulas may have more or less appeal according to brand. As solids are introduced, test new foods one spoonful at a time, one brand at a time. Baby food now comes in a wide variety of flavors and consistencies, and you may need to throw away many barely touched jars before finding the favored few. If you make your own baby food, you may feel particularly frustrated when the baby refuses your offering.

Your infant may also be sensitive to the temperature of foods and liquids. If you have a problem with bottle feeding, it may be due to the baby's sensitivity to the formula's temperature. Try it cooler and try it a bit warmer, and then be as consistent as possible when you discover what suits him. Sensitivity to temperature as well as to the feel of the water itself may also be behind the distress of a baby who screams when bathed.

The Highly Active Infant

Sturdy crib bumpers are essential for the very active infant. The crib itself should have high rails, as these babies will climb out at an earlier age than most. They are also very active sleepers who kick off blankets and move all around the crib. If you have a cool house and a problem keeping the baby covered, dress him in pajamas with feet (and in blanket sleepers in the winter). These are babies who have to be watched carefully when they are on the changing table, lying on your bed, or in the bath.

A note on breastfeeding: I don't know if breastfeeding calms a temperamentally difficult infant; I don't believe this question has been studied systematically. However, if you are committed to nursing, then realize that such infants can make the experience less rewarding. Highly active babies, irregular infants, or those with low threshold, are particularly difficult to breastfeed. Remember that the baby is *not* rejecting you.

The Baby with Initial Withdrawal and/or Poor Adaptability

Although this infant will reject many new foods when they are first introduced, the first rejection doesn't always mean he will continue to dislike what you've given him. Introduce new foods gradually, and try offering the food or liquid several times before you give up. It may take some time to sort out whether the baby's rejection of a food is due to initial withdrawal or low threshold to taste.

The same is true for other new experiences. Allow your baby to see a new stuffed toy from a safe distance several times before you try to put it into his arms or place it next to him in the crib. Be aware that the bottle in the shape of a cartoon character, which you bought in the hope of pleasing him, may alarm him instead. You will soon begin to recognize the variations from the familiar routine that cause upset.

Although many babies begin to exhibit what is called

"stranger anxiety" at about the age of 8 or 9 months, this baby's difficulty is evident earlier. It also persists well past the age at which "stranger anxiety" ordinarily abates. When possible, warn friends and relatives not to approach the baby too quickly and not to try to pick him up right away. Even a familiar person with a significant feature changed—new eyeglasses, a beard shaved off— can cause a reaction.

In general, routine is especially important to the poorly adaptable baby, and with a very difficult infant, you may need to routinize even the details of holding, comforting, burping, bathing, and putting him down to sleep.

Understanding the temperament of your difficult infant and basing your management on this allows you to lay a foundation for his future. You are, from an early age, developing an approach that is geared to his individuality. While you may find your baby exhausting, try to remain sensitive to the expressions of his temperament. It is particularly important at this age for you to have a good, honest relationship with your pediatrician. He can be of great help to you with day-to-day problems, but remember to talk temperament with him.

Above all, don't take your baby's behavior personally. It does not mean that you are an inadequate parent. By adopting a more neutral yet loving approach, you will be preventing the vicious circle from developing, and nothing is more important to you, your baby, and the rest of your family.

11

BEYOND THE CHILD
The Family and the World Outside

In describing the Difficult Child Program to this point, I have focused primarily on your response to your child. By now you are an expert on your child's temperament, you are working to reestablish your parental authority, and you are learning to anticipate and manage behavior related to temperament. Probably your child is becoming easier to deal with, and the effects of the vicious circle are beginning to diminish.

But the change in your relationship with your child goes hand in hand with other changes. Recall for a moment the "ripple effect"—how the impact of your child's problem behavior spread out from the mother to the rest of the family and affected the difficult child's entire world. Now you can hope for a new ripple effect caused by his improvement. This is a time of considerable readjustment for everyone in the family. It is also a time when your attention to key elements in your child's environment can do a great deal to reinforce and ensure his continued progress. In this chapter I will discuss some of the most important ways in which you can encourage this *positive* ripple effect.

But first a word about your expectations. Don't be alarmed if, after an initial period of progress, your child reverts to some of his problem behavior, or if wear-and-tear manifestations occasionally crop up anew. In many children, progress is marked by spurts, regression, consolidation, and further spurts, and this is especially true of difficult children. Parents sometimes find this hard to accept. "But everything was going so well," they say.

Try to be as objective about the unevenness of behavioral progress as you are about the spurts and plateaus in your child's weight gain. Even in easy children, you can see slippage at times of stress or change. With a difficult child, such slippage also can occur for less apparent or even paradoxical reasons; your child may have "caught on" to one of the techniques, does well for a while, but then reverts. Or a rough period may *precede* a substantial—even surprising—change for the better. Have faith in yourself and your child. You are learning and progressing together.

Be prepared, also, for progress that is uneven from area to area. Just as a note comes from the teacher saying your child is behaving much better in kindergarten, you may notice that he has started to pick fights with his younger sibling every day after school. Or perhaps she has mastered her morning and evening routines, but is becoming impossibly stubborn about clothes and food. You will need to be flexible and constantly to adapt and update your approach to your child.

To help you take a longer view of your child's development, I suggest you take time every few months to review the information you gathered during your five-day study period. It is so easy to forget where you started. You will almost surely be encouraged by how good the overall picture is, despite your feeling that there still are day-to-day problems.

I also tell parents to beware of one common tendency, the desire to "make the child feel better." We become so concerned about our children's self-image that we can easily go overboard, constantly telling the child how wonderful he is for the most minor accomplishments. These kinds of "self-image commercials" achieve very little and in fact can easily backfire. They may create pressures and expectations that your child feels he can't meet, and can actually cause behavior to regress. As delighted as you are at signs of progress, do not greet every tiny improvement with effusive praise. Of course you should acknowledge that your child is doing better and let him know that you are pleased. But don't stage a major celebration over a moderately improved school report or a trouble-free visit to Grandmother's house. The most meaningful "reward" for any child is to experience consistently the approval and benign attitude of his parents.

STRENGTHENING THE FAMILY

As you apply the program, and as your negative involvement with your child lessens, realignments are also occurring in other family relationships. When the program works successfully, it actually frees some of your time.

Siblings

As you know, siblings develop their own ways of coping with the presence of a difficult child. They may have felt sorry for him. They may have felt neglected. They may have become "too good" in a pseudo-adult way. Or they may have misbehaved to get attention.

Younger siblings who have been misbehaving often return to normal quickly. They may simply need a little extra attention, and to be dealt with more consistently according to some of the principles of parental authority you have learned.

More may be needed for an older sibling. Acknowledge early on that he has been getting a raw deal. Then explain why. Point out that the difficult child has a different "makeup" and that he's hard to manage. This requires the parent to work harder and spend more time, and thus you have been giving more attention to the other child. But then you can say, "We've gone too far and we're going to change. We've read a book and we've learned some new things to do." Make the child aware of some of the techniques you'll be using, such as the changing clock and the star system. Tell him what you're going to do that's new and different.

Many parents now ask, "But what do I tell my other child about these systems and routines that don't involve him and that require presents, stickers, and other nice things?" Tell the other child that these methods are being used to help the difficult child change his behavior, and don't have anything to do with favoritism. Start to plan special treats for the sibling. Do things with him alone: a movie, a dinner out, a ball game.

Be sure also to explain that the difficult child is not being allowed to "get away with things" unfairly—such as not being required to eat at family mealtimes—but that this is *part of your plan* to improve his behavior and make the entire family happier. If you make new changes, keep your other child informed. (Obviously, the extent of information you share depends on the sibling's age.)

Excessively good siblings of difficult children need special attention. The "perfect child" who has been such a relief to you needs to be released from his position as family saint. If he gets too involved in that role, there can be trouble later. Therefore, after you have settled some things with your difficult child and have established your new systems and routines, talk directly to the other child about how he has felt: "I know you've felt worried and tried very hard to be good, but you don't have to be that way so much anymore." Encourage him to express his feelings. And when he starts to rebel or misbehave on occasion, like any other child, don't be too concerned even if he goes a little too far.

An interesting note: *All* children have a temperament. They are all individuals in their own right, and any child, even if basically easy, may have one or two difficult temperamental traits. Thus you may find that not only the principles of adult authority but also your expertise on temperament may help you to deal better with your other children and to respect their individuality.

Quality Time

What about yourselves? This is the time to work on your marital relationship and to pay more attention to your own needs, especially if your marriage has been strained over the past few years. Schedule more adult time alone. Get a good baby-sitter, and introduce her gradually. Start to go out again. Invite friends over to your home to visit. Get away for an occasional weekend. Prepare the child when you go out, but don't linger too long over saying good-bye. Parents of difficult children tend to neglect their own needs. This isn't good for anyone, including the child. So start paying more attention to yourselves.

The mother in particular needs to expand her horizons. You might take a course, pursue a hobby, see more of your friends, get out to a museum or a movie, or even start to look for a job. When you do go out alone, don't spend all your free time doing things for your child or the rest of your family. Do things for *yourself*.

You might also consider organizing more outings as a family on the weekends. There are places where a noisy or active child would not disturb other families: parks, large science or natural-history museums, a beach, zoos.

In general, you need gradually to replace the pressure in your lives not just with "peace and quiet" but also with positive enjoyment of each other, your difficult child, and your other children. The family atmosphere should continue to improve when you begin to have more good times together.

Television

As you have seen in some of the vignettes, the "electronic baby-sitter" can be a valuable tool in the management of a difficult child. Early in the program I recommend to parents that they put aside their own attitudes about TV watching for children and simply use the TV as a tool in improving their management of the child. Sometimes it may be the only thing that pacifies a child who would otherwise be running wild. It may be the only way a mother can buy a few free moments for herself. Such use of the TV is perfectly all right. Of course continuing excessive use can become hard to reverse. Therefore, as your child becomes easier to manage, you can begin to limit the time he spends in front of the set. Don't feel guilty about planned viewing of favorite shows, however. And by all means leave some TV time as part of a morning or evening routine if this fits in with your family value system.

Grandparents

How much should you involve your own parents and your in-laws in your new approach to your child? This depends on two factors: their flexibility and willingness to understand, and the quality of their relationship with you.

If this relationship is good and the grandparents are receptive, discuss the new management techniques with your family. Focus on the temperament of your child, and educate your parents so there will be consistency in the way he's treated when he's with them.

If, however, the grandparents have strict or rigid ideas about upbringing, you as parents have to ask yourselves how your child responds to them. If he accepts the strictness and it is expressed in the context of a loving relationship, then just let things be and don't interfere. Simply ask your parents not to criticize you in front of the child or to undermine your authority.

But if your parents have a very hard time accepting your new approach, you may have to decide to limit your contact with them while you are getting things right in your own family. Otherwise their criticism of you will work against what you are doing with your child. It would be better to resume close relations with them when things improve for you at home.

HANDLING STRESS AND CHANGE

Difficult children are particularly sensitive barometers to trouble, stress, or change in the family and can easily regress temporarily at such times. It is important for you to be aware of situations that can cause problems for your difficult child. Some of these events are positive, others negative. They include:

- Christmas, Hanukkah, or other big family holidays

- school vacations
- summer camp
- trips
- a new baby in the family
- the first days or weeks of school
- a move to a new school
- moving homes
- parent's loss of a job or financial reverses
- mother returning to work

And, of course, there are circumstances that would affect any child:

- the child's illness
- the parents' divorce
- illness (physical or emotional) in the family
- death of someone close to the child

At such times, try not to *start* any brand-new techniques, or enforce any new rules rigidly. Keep your routine as familiar and simple as possible. If your child regresses, however, feel free to *go back* to certain systems or techniques for a while.

For example, a 5-year-old girl who is successfully performing her morning and evening routines without the benefit of the star system suddenly returns to her old disorganized and difficult ways. Her parents are baffled at first, but when they ask themselves what has been going on in the family, they realize their daughter is reacting to their own changes and conflicts. The father has left one job for another, a switch that has not pleased his wife, and there have been intense discussions and some arguments about it. Most of this has been outside the child's hearing, and the parents felt she couldn't understand the issues anyway, but she has obviously picked up on the increased tension. Once her parents realize this, they can explain to their daughter in simple terms what is going on and bring back the star system until their relationship is smooth again. Some difficult children are more sensitive than others to your relationship as a couple, as well as to changes in their environment.

Positive events such as Christmas, Hanukkah, or a family vacation need to be planned and discussed well in advance. The child may react to all the excitement and change. Try to stick as much as possible to established routines. Reintroduce some of the management techniques, such as the changing clock. Prepare your child carefully for new situations. Familiarize him with your travel schedule if the family is going away.

When difficult children regress temporarily, it is usually by becoming more fearful and clingy, sleeping badly, or misbehaving. Try not to become too anxious, not to regress yourself, and maintain a sympathetic, kind attitude. If you provide a secure base for your child when he is going through a rough patch, usually he will come out of it quickly.

Divorce and Remarriage

New family structures, like the single-parent family and the stepfamily, are common in our Western society. Much has been written on easing the stress of divorce for children. I only want to add that the child's temperament should be considered. *Consistency* is the key with difficult children. If all significant adults dealing with the child respond to him in roughly the same way, by following some of the principles and techniques you have already learned, he will do well. This may be hard for some divorcing couples, because it implies the need for rational communication in what is often a highly-charged atmosphere. I can only urge you to try, as best you can, to keep your feelings about your ex-spouse separate from your relationship with your child.

If the child visits with the father overnight or on weekends, the father should try to maintain, at least to some extent, the child's familiar routines.

If you are a single parent, you have applied the program with some obvious modifications. The only thing to emphasize is that, if you are a working mother, you should pay particular attention to your choice of substitute caregivers.

In a recently-formed stepfamily, your new spouse should participate in the program with you, and the stepsiblings should know about the difficult child's temperament.

A final note: Difficult children, as you know, can certainly put a strain on a marriage. However, in my experience, it is extremely rare to find a situation where the difficult child was the *only* reason for the decision to separate. So try not to be angry at your child, and avoid implying to him in any way that he is responsible for breaking up your marriage.

SCHOOLS AND TEACHERS

Your child's first world outside the family is that of school and teachers and peers. There is such a thing as good teacher/child fit just as there is good parent/child fit, and both are very important to your child's continued progress.

A few words about *when* your child should start school. In our modern society increasing emphasis is being placed on early schooling. The term "preschooler" is not even applicable in some instances. Vigorous debate exists in the professional community as to the wisdom of this approach. I believe that this decision should depend on the particular child. I tend to encourage parents to be experimental but flexible. If you are not sure whether your child is ready for school, by all means try sending him; but be prepared to change your mind if it is clear that the situation is not working out—without feeling as if you or your child has failed.

School and Class Selection

The right setting for your child is not necessarily the school currently considered the "best" in your community (although it may be). Rather, it is the school that meets his individual needs and that will maintain open communication with you, the parent. In some small communities you may have little or no choice. But a growing number of parents are making choices even when there appear to be none, for example by obtaining permission to move children across school district lines. Whatever your options, look at them from the point of view of your child and his temperament.

A very active child ideally needs a school that provides structure but also room to run and play freely. Ask questions like: How much of the day is conducted according to plan with a regular, pre-set schedule? How often can the children get outside or into the gym? Are the children partly responsible for selecting their own activities, or is everyone supposed to do the same thing at the same time? A strong-willed child who has problems with change needs a school with a flexible approach.

In general you are looking for a middle-of-the-road school with a warm atmosphere that combines structure with flexibility, and has a basic philosophy of respecting the individuality of children. Your attitude in making this selection is important: your child is *not* some problem kid the school should be begged to take but rather an individual who deserves the best school possible. When you visit any prospective school for your child, your attitude should be that you are evaluating the school as well as the school evaluating your child. Be frank in sharing information about the child, but also ask questions about the school's philosophy.

If it seems to you that none of the nursery schools you've visited is just right for your child, try one of them on an experimental basis. It might work well, and at this age there's very little lost if you have to take him out.

Selection of class and teacher is generally up to the school, but feel free to initiate a discussion of what is best for your child. Be frank but diplomatic. You don't want your child treated as a statistic, but you also don't want him to be too much a focus of attention. If you know that one of the first-grade teachers is more flexible and accepting in attitude, ask the school if your child might be placed in her class. Some difficult children do better in a small class where a little extra individual attention is available. Always keep in mind that you are taking this attitude not because your child is "bad" or a "problem" but because he is an *individual,* and you want to make sure that his individuality will be understood, respected, and encouraged.

Teacher/Child Fit

You've already seen that many difficult children do better in school with the teacher. However, this is not automatic. Teachers spend a great deal of time with the children, and the concept of *fit* is relevant to the teacher/child relationship. The teacher's experience and the teacher's personality also come into play.

For example, teachers may, like mothers, be more or less rigid and more or less relaxed. The difficult child does best with a teacher who has found a balance between acceptance and structure, between allowing the child some free expression and insisting that other things be done according to certain rules. But there can be problems with teachers who fall at either end of the spectrum. Let's take the example of a teacher who does not bend and who wants her charges to observe *all* her many rules and regulations. Here is a case where an extremely active child is going to have a nearly impossible time getting along with his teacher, as will a poorly adaptable one. When the teacher claps her hands and signals the end of an activity, these children are not going to stop what they're doing at once. They've gotten "locked in." If the teacher insists, she may be in for trouble. Certainly the child will suffer from this inflexibility, the same way he might if his parents were rigid. Such a teacher will also have trouble with the highly intense, stubborn child.

The opposite end of the spectrum can be problematic, too. An unstructured teacher with very few hard-and-fast rules about what she wants done in her classroom can be just as negative for a difficult child. Not knowing what's expected can make an overactive child more wild; not being given any routine can leave a poorly adaptable child at a loss.

A good teacher will give the poorly adaptable child more time to switch activities because she's noticed the child has touble with transitions. She will sense when an active, distractible child needs a period of calm. This kind of benign acceptance has a very positive impact on the difficult child, and as a result he will generally behave better in school.

Whether or not your child has problems, you need to establish a good relationship with the teachers, one that permits information and suggestions to be exchanged. Be diplomatic, but clue the teacher in to some of the issues and techniques you use at home. Remember, you are the expert. Emphasize the child's strengths as well as the problem areas. The vast majority of teachers will be grateful for such information. A teacher with one or more difficult children in her class could get a lot out of this book. Beware, however, of the teacher who takes an attitude of "What do you know?" or "Don't teach me my job."

Also, if during the course of the year you start receiving a lot of notes about your child's behavior or are repeatedly called in for conferences, then something is wrong. Don't automatically assume it's your child's fault. The teacher should be able to deal with most issues without notifying you. If this is not happening, the problem may lie as much with the teacher or the class composition as with your child.

In my practice, I have seen some situations where perfectly normal but difficult children were labeled as troubled or even emotionally disturbed when the reality was that the child was in the wrong school or with the wrong teacher.

School Refusal

Many young children are reluctant to separate from their mothers when they start school. The difficult child may have more trouble, both because of his initial withdrawal and because he can be more anxious. Due to these two factors, the first week of school is likely to be harder for some difficult children. If the mother is also anxious, the situation is compounded, and school refusal may develop. School phobia, as this is known in its more intense form, is caused more by the child's problem separating from the mother than by factors in the school. In such cases the mother herself is usually very involved. She may hover over her child, want to protect him, and be tentative about leaving him in school.

What can you do?

With a preschool child, it's all right to stay at the school for a while and work toward a gradual separation. Follow the pace of the child's integration with the classroom. The teachers will help you evaluate his progress. And at home you can help by reading him stories about brave animals or getting him a "brave companion" stuffed animal.

In elementary school, the most common times for school refusal are in kindergarten and in first grade. Here you must develop an inner attitude that *the child belongs in school.* The child has to go, there is no choice, and you have to leave him. An abrupt cutoff is much better for the child because otherwise you and the child get more and more enmeshed. So don't prolong the good-byes. Once you leave, the child usually is okay. If your child is particularly clinging and scared to separate, arrange for an adult in the school to take him from you—then leave.

In some cases the child gets up in the morning with a headache or stomachache, complaining that he's too sick to go to school. Although the pain may be real enough, it is usually not due to illness but rather a manifestation of anxiety. A good way to handle this is to tell the child to go to school, and if he's still ill in school to see the school nurse and let her decide. This gets the decision away from you and from the issue of separation.

Some things you should *not* do:

• Don't give the child commercials about school. Don't get too involved promoting it: "Isn't first grade fun? Don't you just love your teacher?"

• Don't ask too many questions about school. If your child comes home and you say, "How was school?" and all he says is, "Fine," leave it at that. Don't probe any further. Don't ask him repeatedly if he was a "good boy."

> • Don't worry about temporary regressive be-
> havior. Even if the child is okay in school, there
> may be regression at home. This is a period of con-
> solidation for the child. Provide him with a secure
> home base and he should be fine soon.

If you have followed the suggestions in this book (see
also Chapter 9) and your child still refuses to go to
school, professional help is needed.

PEERS

If your child's behavior has made it difficult for him to
make friends or even to play well with other children,
your new approach should help him in this area, too. As
he is better managed at home and in school, he'll find it
easier to get along with peers. While you don't want to
become his "social secretary," you can certainly encourage and arrange dates with other children, and plan
after-school activities. By educating your older child about
his temperament, you are also helping him master it in
his relations with others.

Remember, however, that difficult children are strong
individualists and that friendship often is a matter of
taste. Some children prefer one or two close friends, and
don't really want to be a part of a larger social group.
Try to respect this. Also, do not be anxious if your child
simply doesn't want another child as a playmate. If she
says to you, "Mommy, I don't want to play with Eliza-
beth," treat this as an expression of personal preference,
not as a sign of social withdrawal.

YOUR CHILD'S DOCTOR

The ideal pediatrician for a difficult child should have
an interest in what is known as "behavioral pediatrics,"
which means that he should be aware of, and be ready to
talk about, issues other than the child's physical health.
If you have as your doctor a family practitioner, the
modern equivalent of the G.P., you may find him particularly attuned to the issues of the child in the family.

Your doctor should also know something about temperament and temperamentally-related difficult behavior. He
should function as your adviser and guide, especially if
you have a difficult infant or toddler, and know when to
refer you for further help. Any time other services are
needed, the pediatrician or family practitioner should
ideally coordinate all such efforts. Of course, even with
the right orientation and the best of intentions, the
doctor needs to make the time available to talk with you
about your child. Good communication with him is very
important. If all these circumstances pertain, you are
indeed lucky.

But before you decide that they don't and start looking for another doctor (assuming your community offers
you a choice), first consider whether you, as an expert on
your temperamentally difficult child, can do anything to
improve the patient-doctor relationship. All too many
parents are reluctant to discuss behavioral issues with
the doctor. They may assume, without any real evidence, that he doesn't know or care about anything other
than immunizations, rashes, or sore throats. Or having
been told that their child is normal, parents may become
too concerned that the doctor will blame them.

Try not to make such assumptions!

Ask for a special appointment to talk about your
child's behavior. See if the doctor is willing to discuss
temperament. Can you help him see that your child is
innately difficult? Perhaps he can give you constructive
advice. Is he sensitive to the problems such a child
causes for the rest of the family? Only after such efforts
have been made and have failed should you consider
changing pediatricians.

SUPPORT GROUPS

Many mothers and some fathers have told me that an
extremely helpful aspect of their experience is being in a
parent support group.

"I felt totally alone until I came to the group," the
mothers say. "I never thought anyone else went through
what we had." "I stopped feeling like a freak." "I finally

found someone who understood me." You can imagine
their relief when, at long last, another mother nodded
and said, "Yes, I know. I've been there, too. And look,
I've survived!"

Since many of you do not live in large metropolitan
areas where you might have access to professional help,
the support group becomes an even more important concept, for it will get you together with other parents who
have experienced similar problems with their children,
and it will enable you to discuss your feelings, successes,
and failures openly. In theory, a support group can be as
compact as two mothers with similar child-rearing problems who telephone each other to provide observations
and encouragement. In practice, you may be interested
in forming a group of your own with as many as six or
more parents. Here's how you can do this.

As you may not have the assistance of any on-the-
spot professionals, make sure before you start that you
are well versed in the principles of this book. Establish
the techniques of the program in your own home, and
see some progress there. Your encouragement will then
help the members of any potential support group.

The best way to find other parents of difficult children is to make up a flyer and ask local pediatricians
and nursery schools to distribute or display it. Use some
of the questions from the questionnaire at the beginning
of this book—ask if parents are having trouble raising
their child, with sleep, with tantrums, with high activity
levels, and so on. After posing these questions, invite the
parents to contact you by phone or by mail. And, of
course, explain that you are forming a support group for
interested parents of difficult (normal but hard-to-raise)
children.

Once other parents contact you, tell them that the
purpose of the group is both to share the pain and difficulty of raising these children and also to offer tips and
advice and *answers*. You will all share in the mutual
understanding of your children.

The group can also serve as a forum for disseminat-
ing information about local doctors, schools, play groups,
sitters, and other subjects parents share in common.

Most mothers (and many fathers) say that the worst feelings they have experienced with their difficult children come from a feeling of isolation, that they are the *only ones* who suffer this way. Getting the support of other parents and sharing information about what works are the primary purposes of a support group.

If your group decides to take further action in the community, you can invite local teachers and professionals who deal with children to some of your meetings. An exchange of information is always desirable. Share with them some of the things you have learned about temperament and behavior. (This should, of course, be done diplomatically.) Parents might say: "We are all interested in helping our children as much as possible, and we'd like to share some of what we have learned and get your input."

It's also important not to adhere slavishly to any program that reflects only what is in this book. Practical, effective parenting is what the program is about, and parents should take the book and go beyond it, adapting it for their child and their family. Although some basic understanding is necessary (and this is what has been presented in these pages), the principles of parental authority and the techniques themselves can be adjusted, expanded, and altered in any way to suit your needs. Once you know the other parents and feel free to speak out, there's no limit to what you can do. And the group can provide you, in some cases, with friends for life.

Tips for Running Support Groups

• To get the ball rolling at your first session, introduce yourself and say something about your child, your family, and your feelings. Then ask the parents to introduce themselves individually and to say something about their particular situation and what they hope to get out of the group.

• Suggest to the other parents that they read *The Difficult Child*. This will help the group to develop a common frame of reference.

• Always set aside time at the start of each session to let mothers and fathers talk about what's happening *now*. These things often are on their minds, and they may want to air their feelings before getting involved in discussing a specific topic or technique.

• Keep it relaxed. You can serve coffee and cake or a glass of wine before sitting down to talk. And don't feel you have to follow strict rules. Whatever a parent has to say about a difficult child is generally relevant to other parents of difficult children.

• As the leader of the group, share your own feelings about your situation before you expect other parents to do so. Opening up with feelings may be difficult, and not everyone is prepared to speak so freely at first.

• Ideally, fathers should attend the groups, although you can plan for a meeting or two without them. Discussing your efforts to work together is always important. Mothers of really difficult children often feel that their husbands "don't *really* know how bad it is."

• One session for mothers with their housekeepers or baby-sitters could be very helpful.

• Give out phone numbers for all group participants, and encourage them to call each other. This kind of support network is very effective, even when you're calling someone only for commiseration.

• Try meeting every week for a month or two, and then let the group decide how often it wishes to meet in the future. Some people prefer an ongoing support group, while others want to stay in touch with meetings every few months.

IF YOU NEED FURTHER HELP

Parents in the program have found support groups very helpful, but a few have also needed further professional help with problems that continue to trouble their families. How do you know when more help is needed? And how do you avoid encountering misconceptions about difficult children and their families?

You should consider further help under the following conditions:

> • If you have a particularly difficult child and can get only so far by yourselves through applying the program.
> • If your child continues to have problems even though you are managing him much better.
> • If problems persist, either for individual family members, the couple, or the family as a whole, even after the successful application of the program.
> • If individual or family problems, mostly unrelated to the difficult child, prevent you from fully undertaking the program.

Once you decide to seek further help, the first step should always be a comprehensive evaluation of your particular situation by a competent mental health professional. Such a person needs to be experienced in working with children and families. Most important, this person has to be receptive to the concept of temperament in order to see the child not simply as an expression of family conflict or environmental stress but as an individual with a set of inborn features that influence his behavior and affect his family. Without this understanding, professional treatment may well be partly helpful, but it will miss the central issue, *the difficult temperament of the child.*

> • For example, if you have a younger (preschool) difficult child and you go to a therapist who believes that children are primarily motivated by unconscious drives, he or she may follow through on this assumption by recommending long-term individual psychotherapy for the child. In my experience, difficult preschool children very rarely profit from long-term therapy. In fact, their behavior often worsens. The focus should be mainly on parental counseling to help you manage the child better, not on analyzing the child.

• Or you may find that the professional looks at your background, links it to your mothering capacity, and recommends treatment for *you*. Therapy for the mother or father might help them come to grips with some personal issues, but they will still be handling the child mostly out of ignorance.

• Or you may see a family-oriented person who will view the child's behavior only as a symptom of family pathology. The entire family, including the siblings, may end up in therapy. Such therapy may help with general adjustment to the presence of a difficult child and with other issues, such as a shaky marriage, but it will not help you deal with the temperament behind the difficult behavior.

• Or you may go to a medical specialist who diagnoses "hyperactivity" (or a similar term) and recommends medication. This may prove effective in lowering a very high activity level and improving attention, but it should never be the *only* form of treatment for any child.

Once again, if the basic issue of a difficult temperament is overlooked, no treatment approach can be fully effective.

If possible, look for a generalist, a so-called eclectic mental health professional skilled in more than one form of therapy. Remember your role as *the* expert on your child's temperament. Ask tactful but direct questions about the professional's general approach, and the goals he or she is aiming for. Such an approach advances a positive alliance between the therapist and the family.

When Does Your Child Need Individual Therapy?

With the older (elementary-school-age) child, the critical issue is whether his "emotional problems" are wear-and-tear manifestations that will subside with better management, or whether the child has been affected to such an extent that he needs professional help.

Symptoms such as fearfulness, bad dreams, clinging, or being easily upset are commonly due to wear and tear and should diminish markedly as you apply the program.

Seek therapy, however, if fears and clinging are persistent and/or severe, or if the child continues to show withdrawal in school; aggressive behavior; sadness; problems in relationships with other children; or, most importantly, self-image problems. In fact, even if your child's other symptoms have diminished, the issue of self-image should be used as a yardstick. Your child may initially have said things such as "I'm bad," or "I hate myself" because of wear and tear. But if he and the family are now doing better in other areas and he still has a problem with self-image, this should be your signal to seek help for him.

The duration of the therapy should be determined by the severity and extent of the problems. An impaired self-image, the most frequent problem found in older difficult children, often will improve with fairly brief therapy lasting months rather than years, provided the family situation is relatively stable.

When Do Other Family Members Need Further Help?

In our stressful modern society, a difficult child can be born into a troubled family. Personal, marital, or family problems can exist quite apart from the difficult child's temperament, with the negative interactions of the vicious circle simply increasing everyone's burden. Thus you may need to pursue other avenues of professional help, either while you are applying the principles of the Difficult Child Program or after you have done so.

If you find that after using the management techniques your child is better but there still are serious conflicts between you as a couple, or if you cannot get together to enforce these techniques, the marriage may need attention, and couples therapy could be appropriate for you.

Individual treatment may be called for if either the mother or the father suffers from chronic anxiety, depression, or other personal problems. Such a parent may find that he or she understands the program techniques intellectually but still cannot apply them. Or the parent may continue to feel bad even though the child is clearly getting better.

If, on the other hand, more than one person is in trouble, or if the family generally is not functioning well, the situation may call for family therapy.

Remember that a commitment to get professional help does not necessarily involve an enormous amount of time and money. In today's mental health field, briefer approaches often are available and effective, be it for an individual, a couple, or a family.

Keep in mind also that none of these approaches should substitute for enlightened management of your difficult child based on an understanding of his temperament.

SPECIAL ISSUES FOR "HYPERACTIVE" CHILDREN

In Chapter 4 I covered in some detail my views on hyperactivity. In those cases where a diagnosis is truly warranted, specialized help may be needed. If more than one professional is involved, a coordinator is necessary. Ideally this should be the pediatrician or family practitioner but it can be any expert professional with an overview of the total situation.

Depending on the individual case, special help may be needed in any of the following areas:

Learning problems: By definition, a diagnosed learning disability requires a clear discrepancy between tested intelligence and academic achievement. However, even in a preschooler, testing may identify a vulnerability to later learning problems. Early screening is being attempted more frequently in preschool programs. Within reason this is a sound approach which can help identify children who truly need extra intervention. We must be careful, however, of prematurely labeling and categorizing young children.

If your child is doing poorly in some academic areas,

psychological testing and an evaluation by a good
learning-disability specialist may define the problem.
Depending on the severity the child may need extra
tutoring, a resource room, a special class within his
regular school, or a school for learning-disabled children.

Behavioral problems and the Ritalin controversy:
The vast majority of young difficult children, whether
"hyperactive" or not, improve with better management.
Should medication ever be used to improve behavior in
children? This is a controversial issue.

Ritalin (methylphenidate) is one of several medications used in the treatment of attention deficit hyperactivity disorder. Other commonly prescribed medications
include Dexadrine (dextroamphetamine), Cylert (pemo-
line), and Tofranil (imipramine). These drugs have
been available for decades, but in recent years differences over their usage in children have sharpened into
a vociferous, often public, debate, usually focused on
Ritalin, the most studied and most frequently used
medication.

Critics rightly charge that Ritalin is over-prescribed
(some 600,000 to 700,000 American children take it),
often not monitored carefully, and sometimes disguises
inadequacies in the school system. On the other hand,
claims that it is a dangerous chemical straitjacket, a
sinister plot to impose behavioral control so as to make
life easier for lazy teachers and uncaring parents, are
certainly excessive and sensationalistic.

Proponents correctly point out that Ritalin clearly
improves attention span and disruptive behavior, that it
can help hyperactive children with their social and educational adjustment, and that it is relatively safe. However, there exists too often an attitude of the "quick fix,"
a tendency to view medication as a specific "cure" for an
established "condition."

My own view is that medication should be viewed as
one of several useful strategies available in formulating
a comprehensive plan for the individual child in his
particular family and school situation.

In general, I don't use medication to improve behavior in children under the age of five. With older children, I use medication under very specific circumstances. Say, for example, that over a period of time an extremely active youngster, one that truly deserves the diagnosis of attention deficit hyperactivity disorder, is in the right class for him and is being managed much better both at home and in school; however, in spite of this, he remains distractible, "hyper," impulsive, disorganized, and continues to have significant problems with other children. In this kind of situation, a trial of medication is indicated, and usually Ritalin is the first choice.

I believe there is one other valid reason to medicate a disruptive child. If the child's family and school are in a state of crisis, the temporary use of Ritalin can reverse the situation and create an atmosphere of greater calm, which in turn will allow the parents and teacher to institute a program of improved management. Once things are going better the medication can often be discontinued.

A child should first be evaluated and then followed by a competent medical professional. The doctor should work in close collaboration with the parents and teachers, so that decisions can be made regarding dose, timing, side effects, and trial periods off the medication. Under such circumstances, the use of medication is proper, indeed, in a few children, even essential.

Other problems: *Language therapy* may be needed. As a rule of thumb, get an evaluation if your child is not using phrases by two years of age. You should also consider getting help if he seems delayed in language development at a later age, if he doesn't seem to comprehend or express himself properly, or if his articulation is a problem. The teacher or pediatrician can assist you in deciding whether to wait, or to proceed with a language evaluation.

A *pediatric neurologist* sometimes is consulted. From a practical point of view, his input doesn't add much unless there is a history of seizures or the possibility of another brain disorder. Be guided by your pediatrician, but feel free to ask what he hopes to accomplish by getting a neurological evaluation.

An *occupational therapist* can help children who need training in fine or gross motor skills.

Allergy and special diets: This is a promising area, but one that currently includes a bewildering array of possible solutions. Food additives, salicylates, artificial colorings, various pollutants, excessive sugar, and trace minerals have all come under suspicion as contributing to behavioral problems in children. Although there is no final proof of the effectiveness of any of the nutritional approaches to hyperactivity, there is a core group of children whose behavior improves with dietary regulation, and elimination of the offending agents helps children with established allergies. On the other hand, megavitamin doses have been shown to do nothing for the "hyperactive" child, and they pose the further danger of side effects.

In general, proper nutrition obviously is desirable. More particularly a sound diet appears to be the key to a healthy immune system. The role of diet and possible allergies as factors influencing your child's behavior should be discussed with your child's pediatrician. Even if the pediatrician quite properly points out that there is insufficient scientific evidence, I have heard enough stories of improvement to feel that parents shouldn't be discouraged from pursuing a dietary approach—provided it cannot be harmful and doesn't substitute for other necessary ingredients in a total approach to the whole child. A reputable nutritional specialist is the person to consult.

Don't be afraid to seek further help for your child, yourself, or your family. And don't feel stigmatized by the need for further help. Not every family with a difficult child escapes some of the residual problems left by the vicious circle. And families have problems that don't just originate with the child. Many of these problems can be helped with the assistance of the right professionals.

CONCLUSION
What Does the Future Hold for My Child?

All concerned parents wonder about their children's future. We hope, we plan, we dream; and, if our child is difficult, we worry about what kind of a person he will grow up to be and whether his life can be happy.

When they first start the Difficult Child Program, most parents are so puzzled by their child's behavior and often are so caught up in the vicious circle that their fears and worries are greatly exaggerated. After listening to their concerns, I generally suggest that we commit ourselves to improving the present and that we come back to the future when things are going more smoothly at home. When you arrive at that point, you will want some of your questions answered.

Parents' Fears

When parents tell me about what worries them most about their child's future, this is what they say:

"She will always be a difficult person."

"She won't have any friends."

"Will he always have these outbursts?"

"Will he be wild?"

"Can she do well in school?"

"Will he get into trouble with the law?"

"Will she always be unhappy?"

"He'll get involved with drugs."

"He will always be selfish (or stubborn or rude or hard to please)."

233

In short, parents worry that their child will remain the way he is now and that he'll get into more and more trouble as he grows up.

As things improve, most parents' exaggerated anxieties settle down, but they are still left with persistent nagging doubts and concerns.

What is behind these?

Many parents, perhaps you among them, are afraid that they have traumatized their child permanently, that they will never be able to make up for their early mistakes. After all, enlightened parents are supposed to know all about "early childhood trauma." Isn't it true that the only thing that *really* counts is how you treated your child when he was young? There has been enormous emphasis on the parents', and especially the mother's role in shaping the child. Words like "rejecting" and "overprotective" have become part of our everyday vocabulary. Serious debates occur over breast-feeding vs. bottle-feeding, the timing of toilet training, stimulating children, spending *just* the right amount of "quality time" with them, and a bewildering array of other issues.

And the effect of all this?

Many of us believe that if we do the wrong thing when our child is young, that's it! He will be affected for life.

This is simply not true!

Parents' early mistakes are not irrevocable. Your difficult young child has not been traumatized permanently by whatever you did before you read this book.

Children are remarkably flexible and resilient. Their development is an ongoing process. A child's personality continues to unfold well beyond his early years. If you were to look at anyone's background, perhaps even your own, you would quickly acknowledge the influence of many life experiences. We all add to our background and basic temperament as we move forward, both through other outside forces and through our own decisions about who we want to be.

The New York Longitudinal Study

You have already been introduced to this pioneering study of early temperament, which provides the theoretical basis for this book. However, Drs. Chess and Thomas have done much more than define temperamental characteristics. They have followed their 133 subjects for a quarter of a century, from infancy to early adulthood. Their study has been highly acclaimed in the professional community for its careful, precise research methodology. They have concluded that both temperament and goodness of fit (throughout childhood, not just in the early years) are very important to a child's development. Furthermore, in accordance with much modern research, the study also demonstrates that a child's future clearly is not fixed at age 6. Many other influences continue to impact on an individual. Regarding the influence of temperament, the investigators discovered that although this persists into adult life, it becomes less and less important as the child interacts with his environment and as his personality matures.

The children studied included "difficult" children, although Chess and Thomas used only five temperamental features to define this category (poor adaptability, irregularity, initial withdrawal, negative mood, and high intensity). These children were at greater risk for problems if poorly managed. In those instances where parents received some guidance, the child most often recovered, and the recovery was sustained. In other words, the child got better and stayed better.

One other important aspect of the study was to show that continuing conflict between the parents, for whatever reason, predicted a greater likelihood of later problems for all children, difficult and nondifficult alike.

One Child's Outcome

My daughter Jillian, whom you met in my introduction, was a classically difficult infant and an extremely difficult child in her early years. She was an initial withdrawer, highly intense, irregular, poorly adaptable, with a low threshold to touch, texture, pain, taste, and smell. She was moderately active, moderately distractible, her mood a volatile mix of negative and positive. There were vicious-circle problems in the family as well. Problem behavior with Jillian included temper tantrums, sleep disturbances, misbehaving in public, struggles with dressing, clinging, and some fearful behavior. She was always easier in school than at home. As parents we had to work very hard with her, often learning by experience and making many mistakes.

Today Jillian is charming, exuberant, outgoing, and happy. She is popular in school and at summer sleepaway camp. Her schoolwork is excellent. She has an incisive and imaginative mind, and brings an original point of view to class discussions. She is very much her own person and will stick to her guns even if others disagree. Her insights are often original and penetrating. What remains of her earlier "difficult" nature? Jillian still is very intense, but she has learned to verbalize her feelings instead of always overreacting. Of course, at times she can "turn it on" like most teenagers. She still has occasional difficulties with the unfamiliar or with sudden changes in routine. Her mood now is mostly positive and cheerful, but can still be changeable. She can be very persistent when she truly believes in something.

In general, as Jillian gets older, she is in many ways a "regular kid," but she clearly has some qualities that set her apart in a very positive way. She is a truly interesting person. I very genuinely respect her—she is a true individual.

"How Will He Turn Out?"

I think you can see by now that my general attitude is optimistic. With successful application of the program, the initial relief you experience will gradually allow you to perceive your child's individuality and his strengths. You will not only be tolerant of him but also will start to *enjoy* him more, to have fun with him. When parents who have completed my program start to speak positively about their difficult child, to take genuine pleasure in him, I know we have succeeded; for this, above all else, shows me that the fit has truly improved and that the child is now on the road to achieving his individual potential.

"But can you tell me more? How will he turn out?" you may still ask. While wary of prophecy, generally I can share with you what I believe. There are three possible paths:

1. The child may become indistinguishable from other children, just another "regular kid."

2. The child may develop problems in later childhood or adolescence, the case particularly with difficult children who continue to be poorly managed, those with ongoing poor-fit and vicious-circle problems, and especially those raised in homes where there is a lot of conflict between the parents (not necessarily over the management of the child).

3. The child who is well managed and grows up in an atmosphere of good fit and parental harmony is likely to function very well and may display positive personality traits such as creativity, ebullience, and empathy. He will be a real individual and may well show leadership qualities.

With regard to his basic temperament, you will see improvement in some areas—but don't expect magic.

Some features can change. Adaptability, for example, improves considerably with better management. Eventually the child will learn to handle transitions himself; for example, he will no longer need a changing clock but will request extra time to finish what he is doing. This kind of internal regulation greatly helps the temperamental problem. Some features have to be accepted. Nothing can be done about them. Your child's high intensity falls into this category. And some features can be channeled into more constructive pursuits.

Looking even further ahead, the very temperamental traits that cause problems in childhood can result in characteristics in young adulthood and maturity that are viewed as assets. Let's look at this kind of possible outcome, trait by trait. (You might also find it interesting to think about yourself or your friends in these terms. How has temperament contributed to your adult personality and choice of career?)

• *High activity level.* The high energy and dynamic forward motion of these children may one day be channeled into athletics. In competitive careers such as business, the stock market, or sales, such energy and drive are essential to success.

• *Distractibility.* The child who moves quickly from one activity to another might become a young person of wide-ranging interests with the ability to switch among them in an easy and versatile way. At the same time, as he matures, he can learn to settle into an important task, especially if he is persistent when interested.

• *High persistence and poor adaptability.* The persistent "locked in" child who resists change may end up locked into an area of real interest, where persistence yields true in-depth commitment to a special field. Scholars, research scientists, mathematicians, and innovators in many fields often display such "one track" pursuit of their goals.

• *Initial withdrawal.* The "shy" child who pulls back when exposed to anything new can grow up to become a thoughtful evaluator of new situations and people, who takes time and care before committing himself. This person will be a good listener and someone who cannot be easily "conned" due to a natural caution. At the same time, many shy children eventually learn to overcome their natural reserve.

• *High intensity.* The extremely loud youngster who tends to overdramatize his feelings could utilize this trait in any area that calls for a "larger than life" approach. Such individuals are often found in opera, theater, film, and popular music, where their star presence and vitality delight their audiences.

• *Irregularity.* The child who won't eat or sleep on schedule will gradually learn to regulate his own unique cycles of hunger and tiredness. As an adult, he may function well in careers calling for odd hours.

Restaurant personnel, musicians, computer programmers, those who write or paint as a second love, late-night employees of newspapers, radio and television stations—all often flourish in upside-down schedules that would devastate their more "regular" peers.

• *Low threshold.* Children with a built-in hypersensitivity to touch, taste, smell, and sound can utilize this awareness in many ways. They almost always have flair. Think what a great chef such a person might make, with his delicate sensibility of taste. Those highly sensitive to color, with what is called an inborn color sense, would excel in many areas of design; while awareness of textures and surroundings is essential to clothing design and interior decoration.

• *Negative mood.* The solemn childhood demeanor that so troubles parents can be a real asset in many professions. Law, academics, and medicine are just some of the areas in which natural seriousness adds stature and professional bearing. And the anchor personality on a national TV news team often is the individual whose seriousness gives weight to what he or she is reporting.

These observations are not meant to suggest that your child is destined for any one profession, but rather to show you that what you now see as disadvantages of temperament could, in later life, become helpful and perhaps lead to an interesting and apt career choice for your child. You can also see how diverse the futures of these children are. By no means do they develop just one type of personality.

The Special Ones: A Dream for the Future

I believe that certain difficult children are destined to be special members of our society. If you were to study the childhoods of people who are unusually talented, creative, imaginative, or dynamic, I believe there would be a higher percentage of difficult traits than would be found in the general population.

I believe that many difficult children have a vivid and unusual creative imagination. In part this is because they seem to be more in touch with how they feel. It's as if their more intense temperament has made them more aware of their responses. The circuits are open and the result is that the children seem freer, more open, intuitive, empathetic, creative, and exuberant. They give reign more freely to qualities of the spirit and mind, and they can be more frank, individualistic, more in touch with themselves and less conformist than their nondifficult peers. In short, the chance for a wonderful mix of specialness and intensity often results with these kids.

Look at the childhoods of some of the most charismatic people of our century, and you will often find evidence that they were "odd" or "unusual" as children. Eleanor Roosevelt, withdrawn and shy, was not "understood" by her family. Albert Einstein was also shy and withdrawn, had no friends, began speaking at a late age, possessed strange mannerisms, had problems with his teachers in school, and was characterized by his parents as "different." Relatives reported that Thomas Edison was "abnormal," and his mother withdrew him from school as a result of his difficulties. Pablo Picasso was a notably stubborn child, persistently dedicated to one thing, his painting. A description of the childhoods of four hundred outstanding individuals can be found in the book *Cradles of Eminence* by Victor and Mildred Goertzel. These people were not necessarily all temperamentally difficult children—perhaps some were—but they were more often than not children who were viewed as "different" or troubled. You can clearly see that this did not stand in the way of their very special futures.

Then there is the story of a most difficult child, a red-headed swaggerer who was disobedient and always in trouble, who was constantly in motion, always jumping up and down, leaping or rushing around and falling and hurting himself. The words "hyperactive" and "difficult" were both used to describe him. He was thought to be "dull" intellectually, prone to frequent colds and skin rashes, an "uncoordinated weakling" with a speech impediment whose school record, one of the lowest in his class, reflected a history of misconduct and failure. The boy's name?

Winston Spencer Churchill.

As an adult this writer, politician, historian, artist, bricklayer, farmer, fencer, hunter, and courageous and eminent statesman possessed many of the hallmarks of the difficult child grown up. He was intuitive, insightful, energetic, magnanimous, and determined, a leader for his age. Yet he was, as well, erratic, inconsistent, prone to mood changes, and sometimes quite immature: he loved to play in his bath, dress up, listen to silly records, and was easily moved to tears. All of this information, and more, may be found in William Manchester's remarkable biography of Churchill, *The Last Lion*: a portrait of a difficult child raised with many advantages but also in a family with many problems, who became a most remarkable man. But he always showed that curious mix of the achiever and the immature soul, the leader and the odd boy.

Not every difficult child is destined for greatness. Each one, however, deserves the opportunity to realize his potential. The techniques and principles in this book will help to provide this chance for your child. Try always to apply them in an atmosphere of kindness and love. Respect the child, appreciate his strengths and abilities, and always remember that he is an individual. As time goes on, who knows what dreams can come true for your child.

RECOMMENDED READING

Ames, Louise Bates, Ph.D. *Questions Parents Ask: Straight Answers From Louise Bates Ames, Ph.D.* New York: Clarkson N. Potter, 1988.

Brazelton, T. Berry, M.D. *Infants and Mothers: Differences in Development.* New York: Delacorte, 1983.

——*Working and Caring.* Reading, MA: Addison-Wesley, 1987.

Chess, Stella, M.D. and Alexander Thomas, M.D. *Know Your Child.* New York: Basic Books, 1987.

——*Your Child Is a Person.* New York: Penguin, 1977.

Coleman, Wendy, M.D. *Attention Deficit Disorders, Hyperactivity, and Associated Disorders.* Madison, WI: Calliope, 1988. (Available from Calliope Press, 2115 Chadbourne Ave., Madison, WI 53705.)

Ferber, Richard, M.D. *Solve Your Child's Sleep Problems.* New York: Simon & Schuster, 1985.

Galland, Leo, M.D. *Superimmunity for Kids.* New York: E.P. Dutton, 1988.

APPENDIX

The data has been drawn from the initial evaluation of 149 families with difficult children referred either to the Difficult Child Program at Beth Israel Hospital or to the Difficult Child Center. One hundred three evaluations were performed by me and 46 by Dr. Carole Sands, my associate at Beth Israel Hospital. A semi-structured clinical interview developed by me was used to gather the data.

I. *Identifying Information* (Total sample: 149)

Age range:	1.0–7.0	
Sex:	Male:	68%
	Female:	32%
Race:	White:	74%
	Hispanic:	19%
	Black:	5%
	Other:	2%
Socio-economic status:	Upper:	30%
	Middle:	50%
	Lower:	20%

II. *Children's Behavior*
(2 point rating: + = moderate or severe problems
− = minimal or no problems)

	+	−
Behavior Problems at Home	98%	2%
Behavior Problems at School (N 111)	62%	38%
Tantrums	74%	26%

III. *Family Reactions*
(2 point rating: + = yes
                 − = no)

	+	−
Ineffective Discipline	92%	8%
Mother not Coping	89%	11%
Marital Strain (N 120)	69%	31%

IV. *Difficult Temperamental Traits* (N 149)
(3 point rating: 2 + = very difficult
                 1 + = difficult
                 0   = easy or slight difficulty)

Terms are defined in the initial questionnaire and
elaborated on in Chapter 1. Note: Poor Adaptability
includes the behaviors associated with Negative
Persistence.

	2 +	1 +	0
High Activity Level	65%	20%	15%
Distractibility	22%	42%	36%
Poor Adaptability	58%	32%	10%
Initial Withdrawal	16%	38%	46%
High Intensity	52%	35%	13%
Irregularity	35%	35%	30%
Low Sensory Threshold	32%	39%	29%
Negative Mood	20%	32%	48%

V. *Difficult Traits in Order of Frequency*   (N 149)
(2 point rating: + = very difficult or difficult
                 − = easy or slight difficulty)

	+	−
Poor Adaptability	90%	10%
High Intensity	87%	13%
High Activity Level	85%	15%
Low Sensory Threshold	71%	29%
Irregularity	70%	30%
Distractibility	66%	34%
Initial Withdrawal	54%	46%
Negative Mood	52%	48%

VI. *Comparison of Very Active and Very Distractible Sub-Group (32) with Low Active and Non-Distractible Sub-Group (19)*

		Very Active Very Distractible (N 32)	Low Active Non-Distractible (N 19)
Sex:	Male	81%	37%
	Female	19%	63%
Race:	White	69%	90%
	Hispanic	22%	5%
	Other	9%	5%
Socio-Economic Status:			
	Upper:	28%	42%
	Middle:	56%	48%
	Lower:	16%	10%
Child's Behavior:			
	Problems at Home	94%	95%
	Problems in School	87% (N 23)	31% (N 16)
	Tantrums	74%	68%
History of Allergies:		*17% (N 24)*	*33% (N 18)*
Family Reactions:			
	Ineffective Discipline	94%	90%
	Mother not Coping	94%	79%
	Marital Strain	66% (N 29)	82% (N 17)
Associated Difficult Traits:			
	Poor Adaptability	88%	100%
	Initial Withdrawal	34%	68%
	High Intensity	94%	68%
	Irregularity	81%	63%
	Low Sensory Threshold	72%	63%
	Negative Mood	38%	89%

Our analysis of the data on 149 families with difficult children who presented themselves for help leads us to conclude that:

1. The difficult children in our sample presented a high incidence of behavior problems.

2. The parents almost always felt confused by their child, resulting in poor management. Strain on the marriage often followed.

3. Difficulties were found in these children on *all* the dimensions of temperament.

We also compared two sub-groups:

Group I: Very Active (2 +) and Very Distractible (2 +)

Group II: Low Active (0) and Non-Distractible (0).

Group I might often be diagnosed as "hyperactive" or "attention deficit hyperactivity disorder." These children have more problems in school and a high percentage are boys. They are more likely to have a positive mood and an initial approach response.

Group II children, by contrast, more commonly show negative mood and initial withdrawal.

The two groups are similar in many ways. Both show a high incidence of behavior problems at home and tantrums. Both are very hard to raise and place considerable strain on their parents. Both types of children are poorly adaptable, highly intense, irregular, and have a low sensory threshold.

We conclude that very active children can clearly be subsumed under the general term "difficult child," and that many, if not most, "hyperactive" children are temperamentally difficult.

Currently (1989) we are conducting a follow-up project. A detailed questionnaire explores the status of the children and families 3–5 years after their initial clinical contact. We are not in a position to present the full data as yet, but the responses received so far indicate that parents found our approach helpful, and that improvement is maintained in a significant majority of families.

INDEX

ABOUT THE AUTHORS

STANLEY TURECKI, M.D., is a child and family psychiatrist and the parent of an ex-difficult child. He is a diplomate of the American Board of Psychiatry and Neurology in adult and child psychiatry. He is currently Assistant Clinical Professor of Psychiatry at Mount Sinai School of Medicine and Associate Attending Psychiatrist at Beth Israel Medical Center. He has broad experience with difficult children and their parents as Physician in Charge of the Beth Israel Difficult Child Program, and of the Difficult Child Center in his private practice. He has lectured extensively on matters pertaining to children and families. He lives in New York City.

LESLIE TONNER is the author of two previous works of nonfiction and four novels. She lives in Manhattan with her husband, Richard Curtis, and their children Charles and Emily.